Does Your Church Have a Prayer?

Does Your Church Have a Prayer?

In Mission toward the Promised Land

LEADER'S GUIDE

Marc D. Brown | Kathy Ashby Merry | John G. Briggs Jr.

DISCIPLESHIP RESOURCES

P O BOX 340003 • NASHVILLE, TN 37203-0003

www.discipleshipresources.org

Cover design by Christa Schoenbrodt
Interior design by PerfecType, Nashville, TN

ISBN 13: 978-0-88177-566-2

Library of Congress Control Number: 2009922558

Special acknowledgment is given to Chris Parks, graphic designer and Tyler
Roberts, web designer, for FaithFull Journey, LLC.

Dedicated to my wife, Beverly, who has loved me with the unconditional love of God; to our family for the joy of our life together; and to my parents, who nurtured me in the faith of Christ.
——Marc

Dedicated to my husband Tim, whose encouragement keeps me going; to Jessi and Marce, who help me stay grounded; to Mom and Dad, who "raised me up in the way I should go"; and to Jesus Christ, who is my Savior.
——Kathy

Dedicated to my wife Norma, for her unwavering support and enthusiasm and to the community of the United Methodist Church that provided me the opportunity and means to serve the church in pastoral leadership. A special dedication is appropriate to Marc Brown for inviting me to participate in the development of this work.
——John

Contents

Resources Online

Step-by-Step Task-Force Facilitation Guide
   www.upperroom.org/bookstore/prayer/TaskFroce.pdf

Strategic-Ministry Plan—Action Plan Template
   www.upperroom.org/bookstore/prayer/ActionPlan.pdf

Church Statistics & Community—Demographic Data Worksheet
   www.upperroom.org/bookstore/prayer/StatsDemo.pdf

Church Statistics & Community Demographic
Data Worksheet—Church Statistics
   www.upperroom.org/bookstore/prayer/ChurchStats.pdf

*These resources may also be found at www.faithfulljourney.org.**

---

*www.faithfulljourney.org is owned and operated by the authors of *Does Your Church Have a Prayer* and is not affiliated with GBOD® or Discipleship Resources®.

Preface

Does your church have a prayer? How would you and persons in your church answer that question? Do you know Jesus prayed for his followers as he prepared himself for the glory of the cross? Do you realize that the seventeenth chapter of John contains the vision and mission of God's Promised Land for Jesus' disciples who followed him in his earthly ministry and for his disciples who follow him in his resurrected ministry? Jesus prayed these words:

> I ask not only on behalf of these, but also on behalf of those who will believe in me through their word, that they may all be one. As you, Father, are in me and I am in you, may they also be in us, so that the world may believe that you have sent me. The glory that you have given me I have given them, so that they may be one, as we are one, I in them and you in me, that they may become completely one, so that the world may know that you have sent me and have loved them even as you have loved me (John 17:20-23).

Every church has a prayer. Envisioning a Promised Land of discipleship, Jesus prayed his followers would live in joy and unity to the glory of God. Living as a Savior sent on a mission, Jesus prayed his disciples would be sent into the world by following him.

Your church has a prayer for entering the promised reality for which Jesus prayed. People in your community of faith can live a vision of faith with which a wandering world longs to connect. They can live as mission people who follow Jesus in his crucified and resurrected ministry.

Does your church have a prayer of living Jesus' prayer? It does if your members can align themselves with the heritage of faith that God has promised to them. A vision of joy and unity can define your church. Your church can move forward in mission to God's Promised Land of discipleship.

Does Your Church Have a Prayer? In Mission toward the Promised Land is designed to help your church align itself to the reality for which Jesus prayed. Through six weeks of small-group Bible study (provided in an accompanying Participant's Workbook) and worship, people in your church will hear, ask, and respond to the same questions as they learn to speak a common language of faith in Jesus. The voice of your church will be heard as persons focus on scriptural principles that are keys to church transformation. In addition, the small-group studies will provide the opportunity for the collection of data that will provide a thorough report on opinions and positions relative to values, vision, and mission in your faith community. This data will provide a snapshot of the current state of your church—the starting point for any effective transformational, strategic-ministry plan.

Through spiritual engagement of the whole congregation, your church will be able to discern its current reality as it forms a strategic-ministry plan that can guide it forward into an envisioned reality of God's Promised Land of discipleship. Building consensus of community, *Does Your Church Have a Prayer? In Mission toward the Promised Land* provides pastors and church leaders with a step-by-step planning guide that equips them for the task of leading their church in a scripturally grounded visioning and strategic-ministry planning process. The steps of this process are divided into three interrelated units that equip three specific groups of leaders (pastors, an Advance Leadership Team, and a Promised Land Task Force) to plan and coordinate a comprehensive process that will allow the voice of your church to be heard.

Through this process, people in your church will learn about the Promised Land of discipleship for which Jesus prayed. They will hear with fresh ears of faith how the story of Israel, standing on the edge of the Promised Land, is the story of the church in today's world. Identifying the giants that dwell in the Promised Land that awaits your congregation, people in your church will learn the difference between murmuring and having the mind of Christ among them. Their voice will be heard as they provide insightful feedback on the current reality of your church and the future reality to which God is calling your community of faith. Following Jesus, they will begin to live in mission toward the reality of Jesus' prayer for them as your church develops a ministry plan that will focus the vision of your church beyond itself.

The experience will focus on the scriptural reality defined in Mark 8:34-35:

> "If anyone would come after me, let him deny himself and take up his cross and follow me. For whoever would seek to save his life will lose it; and whoever loses his life for my sake and the gospel's will save it."

This reality will teach the people in your church the difference between death, crucifixion, and resurrection. Rather than seeking to defend what has led to its present understanding of ministry, your congregation can live into a resurrected future that focuses beyond the present. Instead of seeking to save its life for its own sake, your church can lose its life for Jesus' sake. A vision of the future where God is glorified through faith in Jesus can shape the present reality of your faith community. Your church can live in the Promised Land for which Jesus prayed.

It is time for your church to enter this Promised Land.

Unit One: For Pastors

UNIT ONE

CHAPTER ONE

Fishing on the Right Side of the Boat

Do you know what it is like to fish on the wrong side of the boat? To cast the nets of your ministry into the same water time and time again with no measurable difference? To fish continually in the same vision of reality as your congregation plateaus or declines?

Sometimes you may realize that what used to work in the past is not working today. Sometimes you may wonder if this is what God had in mind when you answered a divine call from Jesus upon your life.

Peter knew what it was like to fish on the wrong side of the boat. You remember his story in John 21:1-14 (*NIV*):

> Afterward Jesus appeared again to his disciples, by the Sea of Tiberias. It happened this way: Simon Peter, Thomas (called Didymus), Nathanael, from Cana in Galilee, the sons of Zebedee, and two other disciples were together. "I'm going out to fish," Simon Peter told them, and they said, "We'll go with you." So they went out and got into the boat, but that night they caught nothing.

Early in the morning, Jesus stood on the shore, but the disciples did not realize that it was Jesus. He called out to them, "Friends, haven't you any fish?" "No," they answered. He said, "Throw your net on the right side of the boat and you will find some." When they did, they were unable to haul the net in because of the large number of fish.

Then the disciple whom Jesus loved said to Peter, "It is the Lord!" As soon as Simon Peter heard him say, "It is the Lord," he wrapped his outer garment around him (for he had taken it off) and jumped into the water. The other disciples followed in the boat, towing the net full of fish, for they were not far from shore, about a hundred yards. When they landed, they saw a fire of burning coals there with fish on it, and some bread.

Jesus said to them, "Bring some of the fish you have just caught." Simon Peter climbed aboard and dragged the net ashore. It was full of large fish, 153, but even with so many the net was not torn. Jesus said to them, "Come and have breakfast." None of the disciples dared ask him, "Who are you?" They knew it was the Lord. Jesus came, took the bread and gave it to them, and did the same with the fish. This was now the third time Jesus appeared to his disciples after he was raised from the dead.

Peter was ready to call it a day after fishing all night. Casting his nets into lifeless water, Peter had nothing to show for his labor. Do you know how Peter felt? If you do, Jesus has good news for you. The risen Christ is letting you know that it is time to begin fishing on the right side of the boat. No longer do you have to fish in waters that yield frustrating results as you prepare to call it a day. Jesus is inviting you to cast your nets in living water where a bountiful harvest awaits. You may even find yourself plunging into new waters of faith as you meet the risen Christ, who waits to greet you in the dawning of a new day for your ministry.

Is your church fishing on the wrong side of the boat? Does your congregation spend most of its time casting its nets into waters that protect cherished memories of the past or cherished ministries of the present? Do the nets your congregation casts continue to come up empty? Is there a spirit of weariness and murmuring as ministry efforts keep yielding the same frustrating results? Has talk bubbled to the surface as people wonder whether it is time to call it a day? This is not the ministry Jesus envisioned for the community of disciples you are leading.

Words such as sanctification, joy and unity describe the ministry Jesus envisions for your church. Jesus prayed your church would be a community of faith that would be known by its mission and the ways it makes God's love known through faith in him. Jesus' prayer for your church and for you is found in John 17. This intercessory and priestly prayer that Jesus prayed for his disciples as he prepared himself for Calvary forms the premise upon which this book and accompanying Participant's Workbook are built: **disciples of Jesus and communities of Jesus' disciples can be transformed as they align their lives to the reality of Jesus' prayer for them.**

Do not be tempted to think that the waters of transformed discipleship will be smooth sailing. Casting your nets into living water will require a new interpretation of reality for your congregation and perhaps even for yourself. Simply patching up your current reality will not work if you want to enter the reality of God's Promised Land. Faithful reports of God's Promised Land will be required for your congregation as you lead a process of spiritual engagement. You will need to hear what people truly are saying about the present reality of your congregation. Listening, you will then need to ask the right questions that will allow your congregation to hear the same message as they have the mind of Christ among them. The congregation will need to lay new foundations as strengths directed by a new vision lead your congregation into deep waters of faith. You will need to replace nets that were torn by an old reality with resurrected nets that will allow your congregation to fish on the right side of the boat.

If you are ready to lead your congregation on a journey of transformation, then this book is for you. Designed for spiritual engagement and corporate visioning through the teaching of biblical principles, *Does Your Church Have a Prayer? In Mission toward the Promised Land* will help your congregation to fish on the right side of the boat. As a spiritual leader, you will engage your congregation by teaching biblical principles that lay the foundation for this transformation. For six weeks your congregation will study the same biblical messages, answer the same questions, and identify the giants that are dwelling in the Promised Land Jesus has envisioned for your church. During these six weeks, the congregation will hear the same message at weekly worship as you help them interpret the reality of a new day of ministry. Following these six weeks, congregational feedback generated through Bible study and worship will provide the input for a twenty-four month, documented strategic plan and action outline for your congregation. The congregation's governing body will review and approve this plan and outline. This roadmap for congregational transformation will allow your congregation to enter God's Promised

Land for Jesus' disciples. Consider the story again:

> Jesus called out to them, "Friends, haven't you any fish?" "No," they
> answered. He said, "Throw your net on the right side of the boat
> and you will find some." When they did, they were unable to haul
> the net in because of the large number of fish.

Are you ready to fish on the right side of the boat?

UNIT ONE

CHAPTER TWO

Sowing for the Harvest

Jesus understood the difference that good soil makes. As a spiritual leader, Jesus knew his ministry was as much about tilling as it was about sowing. Through preaching and teaching, Jesus cultivated the lives of his disciples as he nurtured them on the path of discipleship that would lead them to the good soil of the cross and the empty tomb. Sowing seeds of God's kingdom, Jesus understood that an abundant harvest of ministry would be possible only if these seeds took deep root within the lives of his disciples.

Jesus calls you to be a spiritual leader who understands the difference that good soil makes. As you launch into this strategic-ministry planning process, preparation is one of the primary keys to success. This chapter will give you concepts and approaches that will equip you to till the soil of your congregation for an abundant harvest of God's kingdom.

> And he told them many things in parables, saying: "Listen! A sower went out to sow. And as he sowed, some seeds fell on the path, and the birds came and ate them up. Other seeds fell on rocky ground, where they did not have much soil, and they sprang up quickly, since they had no depth of soil. But when the sun rose, they were

scorched; and since they had no root, they withered away. Other
seeds fell among thorns, and the thorns grew up and choked them.
Other seeds fell on good soil and brought forth grain, some a hun-
dredfold, some sixty, some thirty. Let anyone with ears listen!"
(Matthew 13:3-9).

Jesus prayed for the harvest of God's kingdom as he prepared for his crucifixion. John 17 records this high priestly prayer of Jesus as he readied himself for the cross. Focusing on his disciples who followed him in his earthly
ministry and who would follow him in his resurrected ministry, Jesus looked
over into a Promised Land of discipleship that his crucifixion and resurrection
would create.

Envisioning this Promised Land, Jesus prayed for joy and unity for his disciples:

But now I am coming to you, and I speak these things in the world
so that they may have my joy made complete in themselves (John
17:13).

The glory that you have given me I have given them, so that they may
be one, as we are one, I in them and you in me, that they may become
completely one, so that the world may know that you have sent me
and have loved them even as you have loved me (John 17:22-23).

In this Promised Land, Jesus cultivates the lives of the disciples for missional living as he equips them to live in the holy space he creates for them.
The seed of God's kingdom takes deep root as they follow their Savior on the
path of discipleship that leads them to the good soil of the cross and the empty
tomb. Resurrected possibilities of life are harvested as they live in the love that
led Jesus to the cross. The present is transformed as they hear with ears of faith
and answer with lives of faith as mission people who are sent in the name of
their Savior:

As you have sent me into the world, so I have sent them into the
world (John 17:18).

Righteous Father, the world does not know you, but I know you;
and these know that you have sent me. I made your name known to
them, and I will make it known, so that the love with which you
have loved me may be in them, and I in them (John 17:25-26).

As a spiritual leader, Jesus calls you to lead your congregation to this
Promised Land of discipleship. The crucified and risen Savior calls you to leadership that transforms the present as joy, unity, mission, and ministry are

aligned for an abundant harvest that glorifies God. As the spiritual leader of your Christian community, Jesus calls you to a ministry that will allow your community of faith to hear with ears of faith. To answer this call to transformational leadership, you will need to lead your church on the path of discipleship crucified and resurrected living. Your ministry will be as much about tilling as it is about sowing as you cultivate the lives of Jesus' disciples whom God entrusts to your care. Understanding the importance of good soil, your transforming leadership will nurture and cultivate the life of your congregation in the holy space their Savior has created for them through his crucifixion and resurrection. In this holy space, you will sow the seed of vision that will equip your congregation to live a reality that fulfills the future for which Jesus prayed. The harvest you will reap is a church that is transformed by the vision of **living in joy and unity in Jesus to the glory of God** and by the mission of **being followers of Jesus sent into the world.** This vision and this mission for which Jesus prayed in John 17 provide the foundational understanding of transformational discipleship.

Tilling the Soil of Your Congregation

Does Your Church Have a Prayer? In Mission toward the Promised Land is designed to help you till the soil of your congregation. This Leader's Guide will walk you through a process of spiritual engagement that will result in a transformational, strategic-ministry plan for your church. (You will find a process overview graphic of the *Does Your Church Have a Prayer?* program in Appendix 1.) The companion six-week Bible study series will help your congregation speak the same language as discipleship groups engage in spiritual reflection together. The biblical principles taught in the study can shape your congregation as a community of faith. This will occur as you teach the same biblical concepts and ask the right questions that will empower the mission and ministry of your church, questions such as "What does God intend for your church?" Just as importantly, people in your congregation will begin to ask right questions, such as "How can we glorify God through our life together?"

In preparation for these six weeks of spiritual engagement, choose and engage congregational leaders who will assist you in tilling the soil. As the spiritual leader of your faith community, you will teach these leaders the key biblical concepts upon which this strategic-ministry planning process is built. Enlisting their support as they help to expand the circle of leadership and involvement, you will eventually invite all people within your church to have their voices heard as they participate in a corporate process of spiritual formation. You will extend this invitation as you lead your church through a six-week sermon series that correlates with the six-week Bible study for discipleship groups within your church. The focus of this sermon series (Appendix 2) and Bible study (synopsis in Appendix 3) will lead to individual and church-wide discernment of God's dreams for your congregation.

While discipleship groups in your church engage in six weeks of Bible study, you will be preaching a six-week sermon series that tills the soil of your congregation with the following biblical principles:

> Does Your Church Have a Prayer?: John 17;
>
> What Reality Do You Choose?: Numbers 13:1-14:9;
>
> Overcoming Giants: Numbers 13:25-14:9;
>
> Asking the Right Questions: Mark 9:30-35;
>
> Beyond and Within: Mark 8:34-37;
>
> Entering God's Promised Land: Philippians 2:1-11.

Through the preaching and teaching of these biblical principles, you will till the soil of your congregation so that you may plant the seeds of vision that will help your congregation live in the Promised Land for which Jesus prayed.

Sowing the Seeds of Vision

Spiritual leaders sow the vision of a church whose very existence witnesses to the presence of a risen Savior. The nature and mission of this vision is found in the Great Commission of Matthew 28:18-20 and the Great Promise of Acts 1:8.

Jesus speaks the Great Commission at Galilee where he began his ministry. This home base for Jesus' earthly ministry becomes the launching point for Jesus' resurrected ministry as he commissions his disciples to answer a world-changing calling:

> And Jesus came and said to them, "All authority in heaven and on earth has been given to me. Go therefore and make disciples of all nations, baptizing them in the name of the Father and of the Son and of the Holy Spirit, and teaching them to obey everything that I have commanded you. And remember, I am with you always, to the end of the age" (Matthew 28:18-20).

He spoke the Great Promise at Bethany. Bethany was the village that served as the beginning point for Jesus' Palm Sunday entrance into Jerusalem.

Riding on a donkey into the Holy City, Jesus taught about true power as he answered the call of being last of all and servant of all. It is at Bethany that the resurrected Jesus promises the power of God's kingdom to his disciples:

> But you will receive power when the Holy Spirit has come upon you; and you will be my witnesses in Jerusalem, in all Judea and Samaria, and to the ends of the earth (Acts 1:8).

In both the Great Commission and the Great Promise, the envisioned reality of Jesus' disciples being called to a life of faith in a crucified and risen Lord defines the existence of the church. The Great Commission teaches that the church witnesses to the presence of the risen Christ by focusing beyond itself as it goes and makes "disciples of all nations, baptizing them in the name of the Father and of the Son and of the Holy Spirit." The Great Promise teaches that the purpose of power from the Holy Spirit is for Jesus' disciples to be his "witnesses in Jerusalem and in all Judea and Samaria and to the end of the earth." Through the Great Commission and the Great Promise, Jesus' disciples understand their calling as they witness to the truth of a crucified and risen Lord. It is the seed of this calling that you will sow through the vision of a biblical principle entitled *Beyond and Within*.

Beyond and Within

The seed of *Beyond and Within* is found in Jesus' invitation for his disciples to take up their cross and follow him as the cost of discipleship is defined through the transforming power of his impending crucifixion:

> He called the crowd with his disciples, and said to them, "If any want to become my followers, let them deny themselves and take up their cross and follow me. For those who want to save their life will lose it, and those who lose their life for my sake, and for the sake of the gospel, will save it. For what will it profit them to gain the whole world and forfeit their life? Indeed, what can they give in return for their life?" (Mark 8:34-37).

Beyond and Within mandates that disciples and of congregations Jesus' disciples must look beyond themselves as they lose their lives for Jesus' sake and for the gospel's. This invitation includes the requirement for Jesus' disciples to take up their own crosses as they follow him by focusing their lives beyond their self-focused concerns. In turn, this focus beyond self requires an evaluation of the current reality within which a disciple is living. If self-focused concerns hinder a person from following Jesus' invitation, then that person must make an intentional choice to focus life beyond those concerns rather than within those concerns. This is the reason Jesus states, "whoever wants to save his life will lose it, but whoever loses his life for my sake and for the gospel's will save it."

Just as is true for an individual disciple's life, a community of disciples must live by the principle of *Beyond and Within* if it wishes to be a transformed congregation. Churches that apply this biblical teaching discern the effectiveness of their ministry by how they nurture and equip people to share the love of God as they see beyond their self-focused concerns. The goal for ministry within these congregations is that people may be empowered to live as Jesus' disciples sent on a mission that is beyond the world's understanding of reality. *Beyond and Within* is a scriptural foundation for churches that seek to share the love of God with the world through an outward missional focus.

Missional congregations understand their existence depends upon the transforming invitation to lose their lives for Jesus' sake and for the gospel's. It is this invitation that empowers them to move beyond a ministry of self-preservation. They assess the current reality of their ministry by measuring how they are nurturing people to be disciples of Jesus as they equip them to see beyond their self-focused concerns. Remembering Jesus' admonition to lose their lives for Jesus' sake and the gospel's, they share the love of God by focusing beyond their own concerns. Through this same self-giving vision, they also look within at those things that are hindering them from living as God's called people. Following Jesus' sacrificial example of love, the cross of Jesus transforms them. Rather than protecting cherished memories of the past or cherished ministries of the present, they focus their concerns on how they may share the good news of what God has accomplished through the life, death, and resurrection of Jesus Christ. These churches measure their effectiveness by the ways they focus their ministries beyond themselves.

Congregations that live by the biblical principle of *Beyond and Within* understand that the resurrection of a new day for ministry is possible only through the cross of Jesus Christ. They realize that if they want to live in the vision of the risen Christ, they must first look to the cross of the crucified Christ. Rather than allowing themselves to die as they seek to save their lives, they look beyond to the Promised Land where God is calling them. Remembering Jesus' admonition to lose their lives for his sake and the gospel's, they share the love of God by focusing beyond their own concerns. Through this same self-giving vision, they also look within at those things that are hindering them from living as God's called people. Understanding that Jesus' invitation of the cross is framed within the context of following him to Calvary and the empty tomb, they know that the journey of discipleship is always a journey beyond the present context of their church's life. Following Jesus' sacrificial example of love, they are transformed by the cross and empty tomb of Jesus. *Beyond and Within* is the foundational principle that *Does Your Church Have a Prayer? In Mission toward the Promised Land* sows. The harvest from this seed of vision can transform the reality of your congregation.

Reaping the Harvest

When the seed of transformational vision is sown on good soil, the result is a great harvest for God's kingdom. Jesus taught that the yield of this harvest may vary, some a hundred-fold, some sixty, some thirty, but for people who have ears to hear, the blessing of the harvest is immeasurable. Jesus envisioned the blessed harvest of good soil as he cultivated his disciples to remember the truth of divine love that was leading him to Calvary.

One of the ancient hymns of Christianity, the *kenosis* hymn found in Philippians 2:5-11, highlights the divine love that led Jesus to Calvary. This hymn encourages followers of Jesus to have the mind of Christ Jesus among them as he humbled himself through the cross:

> Let the same mind be in you that was in Christ Jesus, who, though he was in the form of God, did not regard equality with God as something to be exploited, but emptied himself, taking the form of a slave, being born in human likeness. And being found in human form, he humbled himself and became obedient to the point of death—even death on a cross. Therefore God also highly exalted him and gave him the name that is above every name, so that at the name of Jesus every knee should bend, in heaven and on earth and under the earth, and every tongue should confess that Jesus Christ is Lord, to the glory of God the Father.

By having the mind of Christ Jesus among them, Jesus' followers understand the biblical story of salvation is the story of a God who remembered and remembers them through their Savior. Hearing this story, they understand the harvest of God's kingdom occurs when their lives connect to the story of God's humbling love revealed through Jesus. For disciples of Jesus Christ, the blessing of the harvest of good soil occurs when the stories of their lives align with the story of Jesus. To understand the blessing of this harvest, you must read the verses that precede the *kenosis* hymn in Philippians 2:1-4:

> If then there is any encouragement in Christ, any consolation from love, any sharing in the Spirit, any compassion and sympathy, make my joy complete: be of the same mind, having the same love, being in full accord and of one mind. Do nothing from selfish ambition or conceit, but in humility regard others as better than yourselves. Let each of you look not to your own interests, but to the interests of others.

This is the Promised Land Jesus envisioned as he prayed for his disciples in John 17. The harvest of this Promised Land of discipleship becomes a reality only when Jesus' followers have the mind of Christ among them. God calls communities of Christian disciples to the harvest of envisioned reality for which Jesus prayed: a harvest of joy, unity, and mission.

The Harvest of Joy

> But now I am coming to you, and I speak these things in the world so that they may have my joy made complete in themselves (John 17:13).

Jesus prayed his followers would be made complete in his joy. Jesus' obedience to God's vision for life, a vision defined by the humbling, self-giving love that was leading Jesus to Calvary, defined the joy for which Jesus prayed. Christians do not find joy in personal acts of self-satisfaction, but instead in acts of self-giving love. Having the mind of Christ Jesus among them, Jesus' disciples know true joy when acts of self-giving love define their life of faith together. They hear and understand that complete joy is made possible as their lives are completed by the truth of God's saving action through Jesus Christ. Hebrews 12:1-2 witnesses to this common joy and salvation:

> Therefore, since we are surrounded by so great a cloud of witnesses, let us also lay aside every weight and the sin that clings so closely, and let us run with perseverance the race that is set before us, looking to Jesus the pioneer and perfecter of our faith, who for the sake of the joy that was set before him endured the cross, disregarding its shame, and has taken his seat at the right hand of the throne of God.

The good news of redeeming faith is that Christians are able to participate joyfully in God's act of redemption through Jesus Christ. Connected to the faith that has been shared with us and the faith which we share, we are living witnesses as we join the cloud of witnesses for whom Jesus prayed in John 17:20: "I ask not only on behalf of these, but also on behalf of those who will believe in me through their word."

It is through a shared or communal joy in the justifying faith of Jesus that disciples may unite in the glorifying wholeness of God's vision for life.

The Harvest of Unity

> The glory that you have given me I have given them, so that they may be one, as we are one, I in them and you in me, that they may become completely one, so that the world may know that you have sent me and have loved them even as you have loved me (John 17:22-23).

Jesus' life and ministry had one intention: to glorify God. It was this intention that guided Jesus as he prayed that the Father would be honored through the Son and that the Son would be honored through the Father in the hour of his crucifixion. Praying as a Savior sent on a mission, Jesus focused beyond himself. Followers of Jesus have one goal for their life and ministry: to glorify God. Jesus prayed for this as he focused beyond his own concerns to the concerns of his followers. Jesus prayed that his disciples would be united in the glory that God had given him: the glory of living as a Savior who was sent on a mission to let the world know the truth about the God of love. Living as this Savior, Jesus, in turn, has given the gift of this glory to his followers. It is this gift of glory that unites Jesus' disciples to live as people sent on a mission to tell the world about God's love revealed in the life, death, and resurrection of Jesus.

Focusing beyond themselves, Christian disciples honor God as they understand their call as people who are being sent by Jesus into the world. This calling manifests in acts of faith that witness to the power of God's love revealed through the cross of Jesus Christ. By acts of faithfulness that point beyond their own concerns, congregations of disciples can become transforming symbols of God's presence to people who are searching for hope in their lives.

The glory of the Christian life is found when disciples of Jesus witness about the truth of God's love. As churches live in the sending power of God's love, they unite through a divine vision of the cross that calls them to a communal life beyond the pettiness and grumblings that can sometimes dominate the culture of a congregation. This divine vision leads to intentional ministry where mission defines the spirit of the congregation.

The Harvest of Mission

> As you sent me into the world, so I have sent them into the world
> (John 17:18).

Jesus prayed that his disciples would be mission people formed by the sending power of God. The passion of Jesus' prayer for his disciples was that the power of divine love that was leading him to Calvary would form his followers. The biblical word for the forming power of divine love is *sanctification*. Sanctification speaks to the empowering presence of God that helps followers of Jesus live in the vision of Jesus' prayer for them. Sanctification empowers Christians to live in the wholeness of God's vision for their lives as revealed through the truth of Jesus' life, death, and resurrection. It is this vision that empowers Christians to allow the love that guided Jesus to the cross to shape their lives. Sanctification is the vision of Jesus' prayer for his disciples in John 17:17-19:

> Sanctify them in the truth; your word is truth. As you have sent me
> into the world, so I have sent them into the world. And for their
> sakes I sanctify myself, so that they also may be sanctified in truth.

An act of God's searching and sending grace, sanctification describes the nature of God's Promised Land for Jesus' disciples. In this Promised Land, Jesus empowers his disciples to look beyond themselves and live as people who are sent into the world through the power of God's love. It is through sanctification that followers of Jesus mature in their faith as Christ creates and forms them into his image. Through sanctification, they live by the biblical principle of *Beyond and Within* as God sends them into the world in the saving power of Jesus. Living in the reality Jesus envisioned, they understand they have entered God's Promised Land of discipleship when the stories of their lives tell the story of God's love through Jesus.

An act of God's searching and sending grace, sanctification also describes the nature of God's Promised Land for communities of Jesus' disciples. Intentional ministry focuses on ways God's love defines the spirit of churches that live in the sending power of God's love and leads congregations to realize concerns beyond themselves. Living by the biblical principle of *Beyond and Within*, these churches understand that the vision and mission of Jesus' prayer provide the good soil from which any vision statement or mission statement for their church may be sown and grow. Living in the reality Jesus envisioned, these churches understand they have entered God's Promised Land of discipleship when the story of their church tells the story of God's love through Jesus.

This is God's Promised Land that Jesus has envisioned for your congregation: the rich soil that will yield a great harvest as you practice your ministry of tilling and sowing. This is Jesus' prayer for your church.

UNIT ONE

CHAPTER THREE

Discerning Leaders

As the spiritual leader of your congregation, you are responsible for identifying leaders who will be effective in the development of your church's strategic-ministry plan. Like Moses, who led the congregation of Israel to the edge of the Promised Land, the time has come for you to find leaders who will cast a vision for the future of your congregation:

> The LORD said to Moses, "Send men to spy out the land of Canaan, which I am giving to the Israelites; from each of their ancestral tribes you shall send a man, every one a leader among them." So Moses sent them from the wilderness of Paran, according to the command of the LORD, all of them leading men among the Israelites. These were their names: From the tribe of Reuben, Shammua son of Zaccur; from the tribe of Simeon, Shaphat son of Hori; from the tribe of Judah, Caleb son of Jephunneh; from the tribe of Issachar, Igal son of Joseph; from the tribe of Ephraim, Hoshea son of Nun; from the tribe of Benjamin, Palti son of Raphu; from the tribe of Zebulun, Gaddiel son of Sodi; from the tribe of Joseph (that is, from the tribe of Manasseh), Gaddi son of Susi; from the tribe of Dan, Ammiel son of Gemalli; from the tribe of

Asher, Sethur son of Michael; from the tribe of Naphtali, Nahbi son of Vophsi; from the tribe of Gad, Geuel son of Machi. These were the names of the men whom Moses sent to spy out the land. And Moses changed the name of Hoshea son of Nun to Joshua.

Moses sent them to spy out the land of Canaan, and said to them, "Go up there into the Negeb, and go up into the hill country, and see what the land is like, and whether the people who live in it are strong or weak, whether they are few or many, and whether the land they live in is good or bad, and whether the towns that they live in are unwalled or fortified, and whether the land is rich or poor, and whether there are trees in it or not. Be bold, and bring some of the fruit of the land." Now it was the season of the first ripe grapes (Numbers 13:1-20).

God gave Moses specific instructions on how he was to accomplish this task. Moses would identify a leader from each of the twelve tribes who would bring back a faithful report about the current reality of Canaan. In choosing these leaders, Moses demonstrated three practices of spiritual leadership: faithful remembering, faithful equipping, and faithful encouraging.

As the spiritual leader of the congregation of Israel, Moses faithfully remembered what God had envisioned for Abraham as he chose the leaders who would spy out the land of Canaan.

As the spiritual leader of the congregation of Israel, Moses faithfully equipped the people he chose to be spies as he interpreted the parameters of how they would fulfill their mission. He did this by defining the context of their responsibilities. They would provide an objective assessment of the Promised Land by reporting on the current reality of what they observed regarding the land, the people, and the towns of Canaan.

As the spiritual leader of the congregation of Israel, Moses faithfully encouraged the people he chose to be spies. Telling them to be bold, Moses instructed them to bring some of the fruit of the land when they returned from their time of discernment in the Promised Land. The twelve spies followed Moses' instructions. They spied out the land and reported on the current reality of Canaan. They brought back a branch with a single cluster of grapes that was so bountiful that they had to carry it on a pole between two of them. There was a consensus report about the reality they had seen: a land so wonderful they could only describe it as flowing with milk and honey; but it was also a land filled with giant-sized challenges. While all of the spies agreed on the reality they saw, there were two differing interpretations of this reality reported to the congregation of Israel.

Ten of the spies interpreted the reality of what they saw by focusing on their own limitations. We see their unfavorable interpretation of reality in Numbers 13:33, ". . . and to ourselves we seemed like grasshoppers, and so we seemed to them."

Two of the spies, Joshua and Caleb, interpreted the reality of what they saw by remembering God's promise of faithfulness as they encouraged the congregation of Israel in Numbers 14:7-9:

> "The land that we went through as spies is an exceedingly good land. If the LORD is pleased with us, he will bring us into this land and give it to us, a land that flows with milk and honey. Only, do not rebel against the LORD; and do not fear the people of the land, for they are no more than bread for us; their protection is removed from them, and the LORD is with us; do not fear them."

The difference between the report of the ten spies who focused on their limitations and the two spies who focused on God's faithfulness is found in how they interpreted reality. Ten of the spies interpreted reality through the limitation of their self-perceptions: "to ourselves we seemed like grasshoppers, and so we seemed to them." This interpretation of reality may be defined as *Perceived Reality*. *Perceived Reality* is allowing your perceptions of past experiences and your subsequent fears of the future to control your response to the present. Through this interpretation of reality, the ten spies focused on how they perceived themselves as they faced the challenge of the giants who dwelled in the Promised Land. Rather than focusing on the promised future God had given to Abraham, they focused on the inadequacy of their own self-perceptions. Their vision of the Promised Land could not see beyond themselves as they focused on the present reality of the giants. As a result, the spies' present perception of seeming like grasshoppers to the giants and to themselves controlled their response to the future that God had promised.

Joshua and Caleb had a different vision of the Promised Land. They interpreted what they had seen through *Envisioned Reality* as they allowed God's promised future to control their responses to the present. Trusting in God's promised vision of the future, these two spies challenged the congregation of Israel to trust in God's present and future faithfulness. Empowered by their present trust in God's future faithfulness, Joshua and Caleb spoke a different message than the other ten spies. They encouraged the congregation of Israel to face the giants of the Promised Land without fear. The focus of these two spies was on God rather than on the giants of the Promised Land, as they spoke the language of remembering encouragement. Through this focus, they spoke of how their remembrance of God's past faithfulness encouraged them to live into the promise of the future.

While the reports of the spies may have differed in how they interpreted reality, it is essential to remember that Moses had chosen all of the spies by identifying them as leaders of the tribes of Israel. In their identified role of leadership, each of the spies sought to influence Israel's response to the Promised Land. Ten of these leaders sought to influence Israel's response by focusing on their fears. Two of the leaders sought to influence Israel's response by focusing on God's promise of faithfulness. All leaders seek to influence opinion.

As the pastor of your congregation, you seek to influence the opinion of your congregation. In preparing for your congregation's strategic planning process, you will need to consider how you are currently influencing the opinion of your congregation. Are you influencing your congregation by focusing on self-perceived limitations or by focusing on the envisioned reality Jesus has prayed for your congregation in John 17? Through the influence of your leadership, your congregation will be led to a point of decision as it chooses whether it will live in the vision of *Perceived Reality* or *Envisioned Reality*.

One of the primary ways you will influence the opinion of your congregation will be in the choice of leaders for the strategic-ministry planning process. As leaders are chosen for this process, you will need to remember the three practices of spiritual leadership Moses demonstrated as he chose leaders from each of the twelve tribes of Israel: faithful remembering, faithful equipping, and faithful encouraging. The choice of people who will serve as leaders in the process of spiritual engagement is crucial because they will either see life through the limitations of self-perceptions or through the promise of God's faithfulness.

Some biblical foundations should also guide in the discernment of leadership:

Remembering Encouragement (Bible Study Two) was demonstrated by Joshua and Caleb when they presented their report on the Promised Land. Remembering God's encouraging promise of faith to Abraham four hundred years earlier, they envisioned God's promise for the future. Unlike the ten spies who interpreted the challenges of the present through grasshopper-sized perceptions, Joshua and Caleb interpreted the challenges of the present by a God-sized vision of the future. Remembering God's faithfulness that had led them to the edge of the Promised Land, they focused was on the faithfulness of God instead of fear of on the giants.

Ability to Ask the Right Questions (Bible Study Four) was demonstrated by Jesus when he helped his disciples understand where to find true power. Right questions invite dialogue, increase understanding, and strengthen community through relationship. Wrong questions invite accusation, labeling, and destruction of community and relationship. Spiritual leaders understand right questions can engage conflict in ways that result in stronger community life. They listen carefully to the questions they are asking as well as the questions other people are asking when they find themselves in the midst of conflict. Spiritual leaders know that their intent and the intent of other people reside in the questions they ask.

Ability to See beyond Self-Focused Concerns (Bible Study Five) was demonstrated in Jesus' invitation for his disciples to take up their cross and follow him on the path to Calvary. People who have accepted this call to discipleship understand that the current reality of discipleship is always assessed through the transforming truth of the cross of Jesus. This trait of leadership is identified in the Bible study as the biblical principle of *Beyond and Within*. Beyond and Within mandates that the vision of discipleship must be beyond self-focused concerns. It is an invitation for Jesus' followers to make intentional choices for a vision of life that transforms present values.

Leading by the Redeemed Need to Serve (Bible Study Six) was demonstrated by Paul when he wrote his letter to the Philippians from a prison cell. The self-emptying love that is modeled by Jesus in the "kenosis hymn" in Philippians 2:5-11 defines this quality of spiritual leadership. Having the mind of Christ, spiritual leaders intentionally choose to empty themselves of their own agendas as they take on the nature and mission of Jesus Christ. Rather than being driven by the human need to win, the redeemed need to serve leads them as they define their lives by humility and by looking out for the interests of others. Rather than seeking the self-preservation of personal interests, spiritual leaders understand that self-emptying love defines their responses to Christian discipleship.

Choosing Leadership

The common thread that should guide the choosing of leaders is their ability to align their lives to the vision and mission for which Jesus prayed: **the vision of living in joy and unity in Jesus to the glory of God and the mission of being followers of Jesus sent into the world.**

The strategic-ministry planning process requires two levels of leadership. The first level of leadership is the Advance Leadership Team of three or four people who will help define and articulate the desired outcome of the strategic-ministry planning process as well as serve as overall leaders of the process. In choosing the Advance Leadership Team, it is especially important to select people who have modeled the leadership qualities of Joshua and Caleb—an ability to trust in the promise of God's faithfulness as they cast a vision for the future. They are the transformational leaders who will influence your congregation to trust in the Promised Land of discipleship for which Jesus prayed in John 17. Remembering God's faithfulness in the past and the promise of God's faithfulness in the future, they will be able to envision a new reality for your congregation through a God-sized vision of the future. Partnering with you in leading your congregation into the future, they are the people who will speak the language of trust in God's presence as they, like Joshua and Caleb, remind your congregation that "the Lord is with us."

From this Advance Leadership Team, choose the leader of the strategic-ministry plan task force (Promised Land Task Force). Members of this task force will have the responsibility for implementing the strategic-ministry planning process and assuring adequate congregational involvement. (Guidelines for the Promised Land Task Force may be found in unit three, chapter six.) You will have the responsibility of working directly with both the Advance Leadership Team and the Promised Land Task Force.

When you meet with the Advance Leadership Team, provide them with a copy of this Leader's Guide and the Participant's Workbook. Share your vision of how this strategic-ministry planning process can strengthen your congregation as it lives into the reality that Jesus envisioned for his disciples. Review the qualities and responsibilities of transformational leadership. Tell them of the prayerful discernment process that has led to their invitation to be leaders in this strategic-ministry planning process. Ask them to accept this invitation to leadership and to indicate their support by signing the strategic-ministry plan Covenant Card found at the end of this chapter. (A reproducible copy of the Covenant Card is included in Appendix 4.) If they are unable to respond immediately to your invitation, ask them to consider your invitation prayerfully and to respond by a time that you will establish (preferably within a few days of your meeting).

Equipping Leadership

After choosing the leadership for the strategic-ministry planning process, you will need to equip them by interpreting the parameters of how they will fulfill their assigned responsibilities. As pastor, you will lead and equip these leaders as you teach them the biblical principles of the Bible study. (A synopsis of each

study may be found in Appendix 3.) You may choose to engage your leadership
in the total six-week study process or to use the synopsis. The choice you make
in teaching these concepts will be your own, but as the spiritual leader of the
congregation, it is essential that others see you in the role of teacher and faithful equipper of the leaders you have chosen. In addition to the Bible study synopsis, you will want to review the principles of Christian transformation
(found in unit two, chapter four) as you guide your leaders to consensus as
they ask the right question: "What does this strategic-ministry plan mean for
our church?"

If there are staff members in your church, you should be the person who
informs and educates them about this strategic-ministry planning process. Just
as you invite people to be partners in this process as advance leaders, you will
also invite your staff to be partners with you as they participate in this ministry
planning process. Members of your staff can influence this strategic-ministry
planning in both positive and negative ways. It is important for the church staff
to sign the same Covenant Card that your advance leaders and Promised Land
Task Force leaders will sign as an indication of their support. You will need to
review with your staff the synopsis of the Bible studies in Appendix 3 as well
as the concepts of the strategic-ministry planning process so that they may
respond affirmatively and positively when asked about this planning process.
To answer questions that may arise within the congregation about the objectivity of the planning process, it is important that church staff not be members of
the Promised Land Task Force. In many churches, members of church staff
represent the voices of different concerns. For the protection of the church
staff and the validity of the strategic-ministry plan that is developed, church
staff should not be involved in the decision-making process of the task force.

Encouraging Leadership

As you equip your leaders and staff, it is imperative that both your leaders and
your congregation view you as a faithful encourager throughout the visioning
and strategic-ministry planning process. Through your role as a faithful
encourager, you are the key communicator of vision and encouragement in this
strategic-ministry planning process. The synopsis of the Bible studies in
Appendix 3 and the sermon outlines in Appendix 2 will assist you in fulfilling
this role. Each sermon relates to a particular Bible study and will help to connect worship and small-group study as your congregation joins together in this
intentional season of spiritual engagement.

As the spiritual leader of your congregation, you will influence the opinion and response of your congregation by focusing on God's faithfulness. This focus, in turn, will empower your congregation to live into an envisioned reality that can transform its current reality. Like Joshua and Caleb, you will remind your congregation "the Lord is with us."

CHART OF PASTOR'S RESPONSIBILITIES IN DISCERNING LEADERS

Pastor's Duties	Key Responsibilities	Helpful Tools
Faithfully Remember	*Remember the vision and mission of Jesus' prayer for his disciples in John 17 *Choose leaders who will see through envisioned reality	*Qualities of leadership in Unit One, Chapter Three
Faithfully Equip	*Define parameters of leadership responsibilities *Teach biblical concepts	*Leadership chart in Unit One, Chapter Three *Bible study key points in Appendix 3 *Bible Study Workbook
Faithfully Encourage	*Key communicator of vision *Key voice of encouragement	*Sermon outlines in Appendix 2

Strategic-Ministry Plan Covenant Card

John 17 includes Jesus' prayer for his followers. Our church will begin a process of study and listening that will help us to understand more fully how we can live in the vision and mission of Jesus' prayer. To assist in this process, a strategic-ministry plan task force (named the Promised Land Task Force) has been approved. Your support is important in helping the task force to hear the voice of our church through your prayers, participation in small-group Bible study, and response to questions that will enable development of the strategic-ministry plan. As a sign of your support, please return this covenant card to the church office.

Believing that Jesus has prayed for his followers, I will:

_____ Pray for the my church daily;

_____ Pray for the Promised Land Task Force;

_____ Allow my voice to be heard by participating in a small-group Bible study;

_____ Attend worship regularly;

_____ Participate in the listening session when the Promised Land Task-Force report is presented.

_____ Signature

Unit Two:
For Advance Leadership Team

Chapter Four: Invitation to Transformational Leadership

Chapter Five: Discerning Task-Force Leadership

CHAPTER FOUR

An Invitation to Transformational Leadership

Leaders influence opinion. Transformational leaders influence and shape opinion. Leaders influence the present. Transformational leaders influence and shape the present and the future. As a member of the Advance Leadership Team, you are being invited to walk on a journey of transformational leadership that will influence and shape the present and future of your congregation. To accept this invitation, you will need to walk in the vision and mission of Jesus' calling for his disciples that is shaped by his prayer for his followers in John 17: the vision of **living in joy and unity in Jesus to the glory of God** and the mission of **being followers of Jesus sent into the world.** It is this vision and this mission that provide the foundational understanding of transformational leadership for Jesus' disciples:

> Therefore, since we are surrounded by so great a cloud of witnesses, let us also lay aside every weight and the sin that clings so closely, and let us run with perseverance the race that is set before

us, looking to Jesus the pioneer and perfecter of our faith, who for
the sake of the joy that was set before him endured the cross, dis-
regarding its shame, and has taken his seat at the right hand of the
throne of God (Hebrews 12:1-2).

Hebrews 12:1-2 offers a compelling account of the journey of transformation. Part of a letter that was written to people who were on the edge of aban-
doning their faith in Jesus, these two verses are encouraging the Hebrew
Christians to walk in the vision and mission of Jesus' calling. Rather than turn-
ing away from their faith in Jesus, they are encouraged to become transforming leaders of faith as they look to Jesus. Surrounded by a great cloud of
witnesses listed in Hebrews 11, the letter encourages them to model the following characteristics of Christian transformational leadership:

- Connect the story of individual life to the larger story of faith in Jesus;
- Align the values of individual life to Jesus' vision for life;
- Persevere in following Jesus.

As an advance leader in the strategic-ministry planning process your
church is preparing to begin, you are being invited to model these characteristics of Christian transformation. Understanding that you are surrounded by
a great cloud of witnesses, you are invited to witness to a story of faith that is
larger than the story of your life. Encouraged to lay aside every weight and the
sin that clings so closely, you are invited to align the values of your life to the
values of Jesus' vision for life. Running with perseverance the race that is set
before you and looking to Jesus the pioneer and perfecter of your faith, you
are invited to make a commitment to help your church run the race of faith
that has been set before it.

Does Your Church Have a Prayer? In Mission toward the Promised Land is a journey of spiritual engagement that invites your congregation to model the characteristics of Christian transformation. Through an intentional process of
spiritual engagement, your church will learn biblical principles that will provide the foundation and framework for congregational revitalization.
Considering how your church can model Christian transformation as your
community of faith connects and aligns its vision and mission to follow Jesus,
people will engage in small-group Bible studies designed for personal spiritual
renewal and congregational transformation. Bible-study participants, using the
accompanying Participant's Workbook, will respond to questions that will
assist the Promised Land Task Force in assessing the current reality of your
church. These Bible-study responses, entitled "Helping Your Voice to Be

Heard," will also assist in discerning how God is calling your church to connect to the larger story of faith revealed through Jesus. The foundational understandings and key points of these six Bible studies, outlined in the Bible-study synopsis in Appendix 3, invite your church to run the race that is set before it.

Your Advance Leadership Team will guide your congregation through this strategic-ministry planning process based on the foundational understanding that Jesus has already prayed for the vision and mission by which his disciples will follow him. An initial study of Jesus' prayer for his disciples found in John 17 reflects this understanding. Verse 20 of this chapter records Jesus praying for his disciples who have followed him in his earthly ministry and for his disciples who will follow him in his resurrected ministry. The context of this prayer occurs on the night before Jesus' crucifixion as he prays in the Garden of Gethsemane with the shadow of the cross looming over him. Envisioning a Promised Land of discipleship that followers could enter only through his crucifixion and resurrection, Jesus prayed that they might live in joy as they unite in the truth of God's love. Jesus envisioned a reality formed by the truth of this holy love where he sends his followers into the world so the world may know God's love through Jesus.

Built on the **vision of living in joy and unity in Jesus to the glory of God and the mission of being followers of Jesus sent into the world,** your church can enter God's Promised Land for Jesus' disciples. As your Advance Leadership Team discerns how your church will answer this transforming call, the good news is that Jesus has already prayed for each follower who forms your community of faith. Jesus has prayed that your community of disciples will be nurtured in its understanding of what it means to be united by the true joy and glory of his life, death, and resurrection. Jesus has prayed that your community of disciples will be his followers sent into the world to live the story of God's love.

Entering this Promised Land of discipleship requires deliberate and intentional choices by your church. Like the congregation of Israel in Numbers 13 and 14, your congregation will be required to choose the reality in which it shall live. A biblical analogy of today's church, this Old Testament account tells the story of the twelve spies who brought back a report on the potential and on the challenges of the Promised Land. All of the spies were in consensus about the reality of what they observed: the land was filled with giant possibilities and with giants. It was in their interpretation of reality, however, that their consensus ended. Ten of the spies reported that the giants facing the congregation of Israel were too powerful to overcome. Two of the spies, Joshua and

Caleb, reported that God would give Israel courage and strength to overcome the giants. Receiving the divergent reports of the spies, the congregation of Israel had to choose the interpretation of reality that would focus its vision for the future. Like the congregation of ancient Israel, today's congregations also have to choose intentionally the interpretation of reality that will focus their vision for the future. Will their vision focus on the giants that are facing their church, or will their vision focus on the faithfulness of God's promises for their church?

It is the premise of *Does Your Church Have a Prayer? In Mission toward the Promised Land* that God desires churches to focus on the faithfulness of God's presence as they envision the future. Underlying this premise is a biblical principle entitled *Beyond and Within* (detailed in Bible study five). Based on Jesus' invitation for his disciples to take up their cross and follow him in Mark 8:34, *Beyond and Within* is a scriptural foundation for churches that seek to share the love of God through an outward focus for their ministry. Churches that apply this biblical teaching assess the current reality of their ministry by how their ministries invite people to be disciples of Jesus as they see beyond their self-focused concerns. The goal for ministry within these congregations is to equip people to live as Jesus' followers sent into the world to share God's love. How the congregation invites people to share the love of God as they see beyond their self-focused concerns measures the effectiveness of ministry. In turn, these churches assess and evaluate which ministries within their congregations are hindering them from looking beyond their own concerns as they choose to keep, stop, or start ministries that empower the effectiveness of their mission.

The biblical principle of *Beyond and Within* empowers transformation within the life of a church. This transformation, however, does not occur independently. For corporate transformation to happen in a church, leaders should interpret *Beyond and Within* to assist people in a community of faith to connect the story of their individual lives to the larger story of faith in Jesus, to align the values of their lives with Jesus' vision for life, and to persevere in following Jesus. For this to happen, worship, spiritual formation, symbolism, and vision must combine to help a congregation live the envisioned reality for which Jesus prayed. As an advance leader in this strategic-ministry planning process, it is important that you understand these concepts and that you work on all of these fronts to help transform your church as it intentionally chooses the interpretation of reality that will guide it into the future.

Worship

Worship defines our understanding of what it means to live hopefully and faithfully for God. Jesus, in Luke 4:16-21, announced the intention of his ministry during Sabbath worship in the synagogue:

> When he came to Nazareth, where he had been brought up, he went to the synagogue on the sabbath day, as was his custom. He stood up to read, and the scroll of the prophet Isaiah was given to him. He unrolled the scroll and found the place where it was written: "The Spirit of the Lord is upon me, because he has anointed me to bring good news to the poor. He has sent me to proclaim release to the captives and recovery of sight to the blind, to let the oppressed go free, to proclaim the year of the Lord's favor." And he rolled up the scroll, gave it back to the attendant, and sat down. The eyes of all in the synagogue were fixed on him. Then he began to say to them, "Today this Scripture has been fulfilled in your hearing."

Prior to receiving the Great Commission, the disciples, in Matthew 28:17, worshiped the risen Savior: "When they saw him, they worshiped him; but some doubted."

Acts 2:46-47 defines the essence of the early church as the praise of God because worship is the act of publicly and faithfully proclaiming that hope for life is found in God:

> Day by day, as they spent much time together in the temple, they broke bread at home and ate their food with glad and generous hearts, praising God and having the goodwill of all the people. And day by day the Lord added to their number those who were being saved.

Worship helps to define God's sacred touch in life. Is it any wonder that, following the seemingly habitual occurrences of mass violence, communities subsequently join together in worship? Overwhelmed by the events that have turned their lives inside out, people are searching for a sense of order and meaning. People are seeking to acknowledge that the questions of life are not the final commentary on life. Worship provides the opportunity for the finite to encounter the infinite. True worship grounds us in the faith of the past and gives us freedom to express the praise of the present as our lives connect with the sacred touch of God's eternal promise of the future. The goal of every church's time of communal worship should be the same: the acknowledgment and confession of God's power to shape and transcend human life. Worship is the primary point of contact through which a community of faith can help people understand that the story of their lives can connect to the larger story of faith in Jesus.

Spiritual Formation

For followers of Jesus, the goal of spiritual formation is the alignment of the values of individual life to Jesus' vision for life. Jesus' disciples understand that faith occurs when they embody the wholeness of God's vision for their lives. Through this understanding, they seek to live in Jesus' vision for life by remembering that faith is a gift from God that we share rather than a private possession that we own. Living by this understanding of spiritual formation, Jesus' disciples follow his great commandments to "love the Lord your God with all your heart, and with all your soul, and with all your mind" and to "love your neighbor as yourself" (Matthew 22:37-39). For Jesus' followers, the maturity of spiritual formation occurs when they intentionally face the struggles of loving God and neighbor by remembering the whole people God has envisioned they would become through their Savior.

Spiritual formation is both an individual and a corporate experience. It allows the image of Christ to shape communities of faith so that they can, in turn, share the transforming presence of Christ through their life together. Churches that seek to be shaped by the biblical principle of *Beyond and Within* are intentional in helping people to be shaped in the image of Christ so that they may take up their cross and follow Jesus. These churches offer Bible studies, discipleship classes, and covenant groups that invite people to practice spiritual disciplines that answer personal and corporate questions about the gift of God's salvation in Jesus Christ.

Churches that are intentional about spiritual formation ask right questions that invite people to understand who God intends for them to become as they follow Jesus. These churches understand that spiritual purity of life forms as people live in relationship with God and each other. They confront people with the prophetic voice of the scriptures as recorded in Micah 6:8: "He has told you, O mortal, what is good; and what does the LORD require of you but to do justice, to love kindness, and to walk humbly with your God?" Communities of faith that are faithful to the goal of spiritual formation encourage people to live for God's glory.

Symbolism

Jesus taught about the kingdom of God through symbols: a lost sheep, a found coin, the prodigal son, the light of the world. Verbal and visual images of meaning that call to mind reflections and possibilities of life fill the Bible. Verbal and visual images also fill a local church and can cause it to be a symbol of invitation for people who are searching for God or a symbol of closed doors to people who are searching for signs of hope.

Every church makes conscious and subconscious choices of how it will be a symbol of God's presence. If a local church wants to communicate God's grace in Jesus Christ, its members need to understand their fellowship is a symbol of God's presence in the community. One of the great challenges facing the church is translating the image of God's presence to a world where words and symbols change rapidly from one culture and one community to another. Perhaps the best way for a local church to translate the gospel to its community is for its members to realize that a local church's buildings, members, and ministries are constant symbols of the eternity of God's presence in a changing world.

Society understands itself in terms of symbols. It is how companies communicate themselves. It is how people define institutions. Symbols may be visible pictures or signs. Symbols also may be mental pictures formed through words. Symbols can be positive or negative forms of communication. Local churches must understand the importance of symbols if they are going to communicate positively the good news of Jesus Christ. Most churches worship with the symbol of a cross reminding worshipers of the gift and cost of salvation. Most churches celebrate sacraments or other signs of remembrance that are symbols of God's presence in the midst of the worshiping community. All churches must interpret and become symbols of God's love to a society that understands itself in terms of symbols. They must understand that their purpose is to point beyond themselves as they connect to a story that is larger than the life of their own community of faith. Churches that understand the importance of symbolism have no difficulty in understanding what Jesus meant when he said:

> "You are the light of the world. A city built on a hill cannot be hid. No one after lighting a lamp puts it under the bushel basket, but on the lampstand, and it gives light to all in the house. In the same way, let your light shine before others, so that they may see your good works and give glory to your Father in heaven" (Matthew 5:14-16).

If a local church is going to excel in sharing the gospel, its members must choose to be symbols of hope and light for a world that is desperately searching for any sign of meaning in the midst of darkness. They understand that the community knows their church through its acts of faithfulness to God's eternal message of love in Jesus.

Vision

Hebrews 12:2 teaches that disciples of Jesus live by the vision of looking to Jesus, the pioneer and perfecter of our faith. It is this vision that helps communities of Jesus' disciples look forward to a new destination for their ministry together as they follow Jesus. It is the vision of Jesus that can empower communities of Jesus' followers to take up their cross as they persevere. The vision of Jesus can encourage a community of faith to make intentional choices that will allow them to live in a future that is different from their past.

Churches that live by the vision of looking to Jesus travel a journey of faith that will guide them to God's Promised Land for Jesus' disciples. Knowing that Jesus has prayed for them, they understand the difference that joy and unity make as they let the truth of God's love in Jesus form them. Knowing that Jesus has prayed for them, they follow Jesus by living as God's sent people in the world.

Churches that live by the vision of looking to Jesus understand that the story of the congregation of Israel in Numbers 13 and 14 is the story of congregations in today's world. They realize that the fearful report of the ten spies regarding the Promised Land was fulfilled as Israel wandered for forty years in a fearful vision of the giants who dwelled in the Promised Land. They also realize that the faithful report of Joshua and Caleb was fulfilled as these two spies led a new generation into the Promised Land. Churches that live by the vision of looking to Jesus understand that God's judgment allows us to live in *our* vision of life and that God's grace allows us to live in *God's* vision for life. Knowing this, they choose to live in God's vision as they dwell in God's Promised Land for Jesus' disciples as joy and unity define their congregation's life together.

An Invitation to Transformational Leadership

Does Your Church Have a Prayer? In Mission toward the Promised Land will help your congregation choose to live in the vision of God's Promised Land for Jesus' disciples. Through small-group Bible study and in public gatherings of your congregation's members and friends, your church will discuss the questions that are being asked in informal meetings that are held in the parking lot, Sunday school rooms, over the telephone, and through e-mails. The study will accomplish this by using tools developed specifically to help your Promised Land Task Force to:

- Engage your church in worship and Bible study;
- Understand God's Promised Reality for your congregation;
- Assess your church's current reality;
- Ask the right questions as you build consensus on interpreting the reality your congregation is facing in a way that glorifies God through Jesus Christ;
- Help your community of disciples accept Christ's invitation to a life that focuses beyond themselves;
- Empower your church to live in the Promised Land of discipleship that focuses the ministry of your church beyond itself.

For this process of spiritual engagement to happen, your leadership team will need to model the attributes of Christian transformation that are defined in Hebrews 12:1-2. Remembering that Jesus has already prayed for each person who forms your leadership team, the story of your faith together must be connected to the larger story of faith revealed through Jesus. Aligning your values to the vision and mission of Jesus' prayer for his disciples, you will need to persevere in following Jesus as you invite your congregation either to enter God's Promised Land for Jesus' disciples or to live more fully in this envisioned reality.

Your covenant of leadership will include intentional times of prayer and study as your pastor leads your task force in a review of the synopsis of Bible studies found in Appendix 3 or leads you through the Bible study participant's guide. As core leaders, you will want to give particular attention to how you can model the leadership qualities that are included in the following Bible studies:

Bible Study Two

Remembering Encouragement was demonstrated by Joshua and Caleb, who remembered God's promise of faith to Abraham as they envisioned God's promise for the future. Remembering God's faithfulness, they encouraged the congregation of Israel to enter the Promised Land.

Bible Study Four

Ability to Ask the Right Questions was demonstrated by Jesus when he helped his disciples to understand where true power is found. Spiritual leaders understand right questions lead to dialogue that strengthens the community. They know their intent and the intent of other people resides in the questions that are asked.

Bible Study Five

Ability to See Beyond Self-Focused Concerns was demonstrated in Jesus' invitation for his disciples to take up their cross and follow him on the path to Calvary. Spiritual leaders understand that the current reality of discipleship is always assessed through the transforming truth of the cross of Jesus.

Bible Study Six

Leading by the Redeemed Need to Serve was demonstrated by Paul when he wrote his letter to the Philippians from a prison cell. Spiritual leaders intentionally choose to empty themselves of their own agendas as they take on the nature and mission of Jesus Christ. Rather than being driven by the human need to win, they are led by the redeemed need to serve.

Discerning Your Team

In addition to personally modeling these leadership qualities, you will collaborate with your pastor through the leadership discernment processes that are practiced in your church to recognize people who can model these leadership qualities as members of the Promised Land Task Force. As you consider leadership for the task force, review the specific job responsibilities of task-force members as detailed in unit three, chapter six. The recommended number of people to compose your Promised Land Task Force is twelve, inclusive of your Advance Leadership Team.

After people have been invited to complete the membership of the Promised Land Task Force, members of your Advance Leadership Team will meet with them either individually or as a group. In meeting with potential task-force members, share with them your enthusiasm for this possibility for your church. Invite them to accept the leadership position as defined by their specific job responsibility on the task force. Define the expectations of their leadership as they covenant with you to model the leadership qualities of remembering encouragement, asking the right questions, seeing beyond self-focused concerns, and leading by the redeemed need to serve. Share with them the parameters of responsibilities as detailed in unit three as the Promised Land Task Force assesses the current reality of your church, develops a strategic-ministry plan with measurable outcomes, and then presents the ministry plan to the congregation.

When members of the Promised Land Task Force have been identified, you (Advance Leadership Team) and your pastor will present the strategic-ministry planning process, along with recommended people for the task force, to your church's governing body for approval. (Chapter ten of unit three provides suggestions for how your presentation may be made.)

Although the recommended Promised Land Task Force membership is twelve, you may recommend fewer if your church membership is small, or you may add additional people as desired. The Promised Land Task Force should not number less than seven or more than sixteen. After approval for the process and task-force membership has been given, the work of the Promised Land Task Force will begin as you engage your church through an invitation to transformational leadership.

Does your church have a prayer? The answer is a faith-affirming *yes*! Jesus has already prayed it for you. Your church can live in joy and unity to the glory of God. The mission of your church can empower people to be sent into the world as followers of Jesus. This is the Promised Land of discipleship for which Jesus prayed. This is the envisioned reality of transformational leadership.

In responding to this envisioned reality, you are invited to make the following prayer your team's covenant prayer as you witness to a story of faith that is bigger than your life, align the values of your life to Jesus' vision for life, and persevere as you lead by following Jesus:

> Holy God, you created us out of your love for humankind. It is out of your love for us that we have accepted your grace and chosen to follow Jesus, proclaiming the risen Christ. As Jesus' disciples, we know it is your desire for all the people of the world to be reconciled with you and one another for the redemption of all creation.
>
> We gather as your people now and give you thanks and praise for your presence in our lives. We give thanks for the ways in which you have guided and blessed this congregation. We too seek your will and guidance. Holy God, we gather to listen and discern together as we covenant to follow Jesus for your glory. Amen.

UNIT TWO

CHAPTER FIVE

Discerning Task-Force Leadership

Your Advance Leadership Team has the responsibility of assisting with the selection of people to serve on the Promised Land Task Force. You will want to choose those who have the ability to align themselves to the strategic-ministry planning process that is this Leader's Guide details. The leaders who are chosen will differ in strengths, gifts, and personalities, but all of them must have the ability to work toward the goal for which the Promised Land Task Force is called: forming a strategic-ministry plan that will align your church to the vision and mission of Jesus' prayer for his disciples. The desired outcome of this strategic-ministry plan will be the realization of Jesus' prayer in your church as people live in joy and unity in Jesus to the glory of God and as followers of Jesus sent into the world. In choosing task-force leadership, it is important to remember that the desired outcome is to select people who are able to align themselves to the same goal even though they may differ in gifts, strengths, and personalities. Acts 13:1-3 provides an example of how persons from differing perspectives can be aligned toward the same goal:

> Now in the church at Antioch there were prophets and teachers: Barnabas, Simeon who was called Niger, Lucius of Cyrene, Manaen a member of the court of Herod the ruler, and Saul. While they were worshiping the Lord and fasting, the Holy Spirit said, "Set

apart for me Barnabas and Saul for the work to which I have called
them." Then after fasting and praying they laid their hands on them
and sent them off (Acts 13:1-3).

Paul and Barnabas were as different as night and day. They had differing
gifts, strengths, and personalities, but they had one thing in common. They
were able to align their lives to the task to which God had called them, and
they became the first missionary team of the church.

The ministry of Barnabas was extravagant with grace-filled encouragement.
Barnabas' birth name was Joseph, but the apostles gave Barnabas the name by
which he would be known after he provided the lead gift in the early church's
first financial commitment campaign. In Acts 4:36, Joseph was called Barnabas,
"Son of Encouragement," following his generosity in selling a field and giving the
proceeds to the apostles. Barnabas vouched for the validity of Saul's conversion
as he stood by Saul's side before the leaders of the Jerusalem church. Barnabas
had the gift of nurturing encouragement that envisions the possibilities of God's
presence in the life of the church and in the lives of people.

Paul's ministry had a different emphasis from Barnabas' ministry. Where
Barnabas saw grace-filled possibilities, Paul saw the need for grace-demanding
accountability. Paul's birth name was Saul. In Acts 13:9, Paul received the name
by which he would be known after Barnabas and he became the first appointed
missionaries of the church. On this mission trip, they traveled to Paphos where
the proconsul, Sergius Paulus, summoned Barnabas and Saul so that he might
hear the word of God. A magician named Elymas confronted Barnabas and Saul
in an attempt to prevent Sergius from hearing the gospel message. Saul became
known as Paul when he confronted Elymas with these words: "You son of the
devil, you enemy of all righteousness, full of all deceit and villainy, will you not
stop making crooked the straight paths of the Lord?" (Acts 13:10). Paul's ministry was driven by the gift of unapologetic truth-telling. Through this grace-
filled gift, Paul equipped his churches and his fellow workers to live in the
present responsibility and accountability of their ministry.

It was the reality of these two grace-filled ministries that led the early
church to discern that God was calling Barnabas and Paul to be the first missionaries of the church. There are many biblical accounts of how leaders are
chosen: Jesus choosing his disciples, Gideon choosing three hundred, Samuel
choosing David. Each story is unique, but each story bears a common thread
as God guided the discernment process: people were chosen who had the ability to align themselves to the vision and mission to which they were called.

Just as Barnabas and Paul were selected for the first missionary trip, select people who are active in the worshiping life of your congregation. Just as Barnabas and Paul were set apart for the responsibilities of their mission trip, choose people who are able to devote their time to the responsibilities of the task force. Listen for the voice of God through other people. Select people who will follow God's calling to be missionaries as they seek to live in Jesus' envisioned reality for his disciples. Choose leaders who are willing to accept God's calling to travel into new possibilities of ministry for your church.

It is important that the Advance Leadership Team and your pastor be in consensus regarding this desired outcome as you select people who will have the ability to bring a faithful report to your congregation about God's Promised Land for Jesus' disciples. In your process of discernment, remember that the desired outcome of the Promised Land Task Force's ministry will be the alignment of your church to the envisioned reality for which Jesus prayed for his disciples. For purposes of group processing and for the symbolic significance related to the number of spies who brought a report about the Promised Land to the congregation of Israel, the suggested membership of the Promised Land Task Force is twelve (including the Advance Leadership Team). Due to the scope of work required, it is recommended that there be a minimum of seven members. Larger churches will want to limit the number of participants to no more than sixteen. The task force will have the following ministry positions in addition to your Advance Leadership Team: task-force chair, prayer leader, communications leader, small-group Bible study coordinator, data coordinator, and mission-statement-team chair. Remaining task-force members will serve as at-large members. In presenting the suggested people for task-force membership to your church's governing body, provide for the possibility of additional nominations.

As Promised Land Task Force leaders are chosen, be aware of the voices of different concerns in your church that the task force will need to hear. You may not be able to include people who represent all of the voices in your church. It is important, however, that your task force represent a cross-section of leaders who will help you to hear and be heard by the different concerns in your church. In unit three, chapter eight, you will find a list of possible voices or tribes that may be considered by task-force leadership to assist in congregational consensus. Following the model of discernment shown in the choice of Barnabas and Paul, your task force should include people who are grace-filled, nurturing encouragers as well as people who are grace-filled equippers and unapologetic truth-tellers. Some of these people will know the stories of your church because they have been members for a great length of time. Some of these people will be recent newcomers to your church. All of the people you select will need to model the same leadership qualities you have agreed to model: remembering encouragement, ability to ask the right questions, ability to see beyond self-focused concerns, and leading by the redeemed need to serve.

Some of the leadership traits you may wish to look for include the following:

- Demonstrate a mature faith and expressed desire for church health and renewal;
- Show they are people who believe in the power of prayer;
- Demonstrate an ability and desire to lead;
- Gain respect from the congregation;
- Prove to have sufficient time available to see the process through to completion;
- Show a healthy attitude working with change;
- Establish the ability to work with persons who have differing opinions;
- Have knowledgeable of your members' gifts and graces;
- Demonstrate responsibility;
- Have the ability to see the larger, longer view of the church.

To assist your discernment, consider people who can best fulfill the responsibilities of the task-force positions below:

- Task-Force Chair—Primary responsibility is to guide the task force in its work.
- Prayer Leader—Primary responsibility is to coordinate church-wide prayer for the task force as it completes its responsibilities and for the church as it engages in the strategic-ministry planning process.
- Communications Leader—Primary responsibility is to coordinate communications.
- Small-Group Bible Study Coordinator—Primary responsibility is to recruit small-group Bible study guides who will lead the weekly Bible studies and facilitate discussion based on the three sets of questions that are provided at the end of each Bible study.
- Data Coordinator—Primary responsibility is to receive and transmit data that will assist in the assessment of the current reality of your church. One source of data will include statistical information that reflects the three to five-year history of your church through worship

attendance, participation in discipleship-formation classes, church membership, worship offerings, etc. A second source of data will include demographic information about your surrounding community such as population composition, surrounding churches, schools, etc. (An information tool to assist in the gathering of this statistical and demographic data relating to your church is found online at www.upperroom.org/bookstore/prayer/ChurchStats.pdf. A tool which will help you gather information regarding your community is found at www.upperroom.org/bookstore/prayer/StatsDemo.pdf. Both tools are also available at www.faithfulljourney.org.) A third and critical source of data will be the assessment of small-group Bible study responses to the sets of questions entitled, "Helping Your Voice to Be Heard." The Data Coordinator will compile these weekly responses as they are forwarded from the Small-Group Bible Study Coordinator. (Appendix 8 contains a data information tool that will assist the data coordinator with the compilation of this information.) A team of task-force members will be responsible for interpreting the current reality of your church based on these responses. (Appendix 9 contains information about a resource that can assist this team with their interpretation of this material.)

- Mission-Statement-Team Chair—Primary responsibility is to lead a Mission-Statement Team in the evaluation and possible revision of the church's current mission statement (if written) or the formation of a mission statement if one does not currently exist.

- At-Large Members—Thes people represent voices of the church that need to be heard through the composition of your task-force leadership. Their primary responsibility is to enable a cross-section of your church to be heard and invested in the strategic-ministry planning process.

In selecting the leadership for the Promised Land Task Force, remember that the desired outcome of the task force's ministry is the alignment of your church to the envisioned reality of Jesus' prayer in John 17. Following the selection of Promised Land Task Force leaders, you will present this vision to your church's governing body along with a potential list of task-force members through a process described in unit three, chapter seven. As you begin your ministry of discerning, remember the vision Jesus has already discerned for the community of disciples who form your church. Like Barnabas and Paul, remember that God has called you and set you apart to nurture and equip your church on its journey to God's Promised Land for Jesus' disciples.

Unit Three:
For Promised Land Task Force

UNIT THREE

CHAPTER SIX

Equipping the Task Force

The Promised Land Task Force has the responsibility of providing a faithful report of Jesus' prayer for his disciples to your church. This prayer is found in John 17 as Jesus prepares himself for his crucifixion by praying for his disciples who followed him in his earthly ministry and his disciples who would follow him in his resurrected ministry. As your task force moves forward with this responsibility, you will share a vision of this Promised Land of discipleship with your church. Like the spies who brought a report of the Promised Land to the congregation of Israel in Numbers 13 and 14, you will bring a report to your congregation. In order for your report to be faithful to the reality for which Jesus prayed, members of the task force must agree that Jesus' vision and mission of discipleship will be the foundation of your ministry together. To achieve consensus, your task force will need to ask the right question, "What does this strategic-ministry plan mean for our church?" In completing this task, you will discern how God is calling your congregation to live out God's will as a community of faith. Romans 12:1-8 provides the framework for living out your calling and work as the Promised Land Task Force for your church:

I appeal to you therefore, brothers and sisters, by the mercies of God, to present your bodies as a living sacrifice, holy and acceptable to God, which is your spiritual worship. Do not be conformed to this world, but be transformed by the renewing of your minds, so that you may discern what is the will of God—what is good and acceptable and perfect.

For by the grace given to me I say to everyone among you not to think of yourself more highly than you ought to think, but to think with sober judgment, each according to the measure of faith that God has assigned. For as in one body we have many members, and not all the members have the same function, so we, who are many, are one body in Christ, and individually we are members one of another. We have gifts that differ according to the grace given to us: prophecy, in proportion to faith; ministry, in ministering; the teacher, in teaching; the exhorter, in exhortation; the giver, in generosity; the leader, in diligence; the compassionate, in cheerfulness.

God's gifts lead to transformation. As you faithfully use the gifts God has given you to discern what is good and acceptable and perfect, transformation becomes reality. As the members of your Promised Land Task Force are collectively faithful to the gifts God has given them, a transformational, strategic-ministry plan for your church will become reality. To accomplish this goal, members of the task force must agree with the desired outcome of your work together: presenting a strategic-ministry plan that will align your church to the envisioned reality for which Jesus prayed for his disciples in John 17. In this envisioned reality, the vision of living in joy and unity nurtures the disciples whom the Spirit equips to be followers of Jesus sent into the world. Transformation will require of your Promised Land Task Force four traits of leadership as you work together. These traits, considered in your selection as members of the task force, are:

- **Remembering Encouragement (Bible Study Two)**—This leadership quality encourages people to focus on the promise of God's faithfulness as they face the challenges of the present and the future.

- **Ability to Ask the Right Questions (Bible Study Four)**—This leadership quality invites people to engage in dialogue that strengthens community.

- **Ability to See beyond Self-Focused Concerns (Bible Study Five)**—This leadership quality understands that the current reality of discipleship is always assessed through the transforming truth of the cross of Jesus.

- **Leading by the Redeemed Need to Serve (Bible Study Six)**—
  This leadership quality is exhibited by people whose lives are defined
  by humility as they look out for the interests of others.

Modeling these traits of leadership, your Promised Land Task Force will
also need to achieve consensus that the biblical foundation that will guide your
work is the principle of *Beyond and Within*. This principle (detailed in Bible
study five) calls a congregation to look beyond itself and understand that Jesus'
self-giving love as revealed through the cross is the reason for its existence.
This key foundation allows Christians to understand that joy is the result of a
life that witnesses beyond itself. Christians do not find joy in personal acts of
self-satisfaction. Instead, they find joy in the truth of God's redeeming act of
love through Jesus Christ. The goal of your Promised Land Task Force is to
develop a ministry plan that will align life within your congregation to the joyful mission of living as Jesus' followers sent into the world.

To accomplish this goal, your pastor will lead your task force through a
time of spiritual preparation as you begin your work together. This time of
spiritual preparation will include a review of the biblical principles taught in a
six-week, small-group Bible study in your congregation. Your task force should
understand and affirm these biblical principles because the strategic-ministry
planning process uses them as its basis. Your Promised Land Task Force will
receive feedback from participants in these Bible studies that will enable its
members to hear the voice of your congregation as you develop your plan.
These responses will represent different voices of concern within your church.
While there may be many differing voices within your congregation, the Bible
studies will help all voices of your church to look beyond their own concerns
by asking the same question when you present the strategic-ministry plan to
the church. That same right question will be, "What does this strategic-ministry plan mean for our church?"

As people unite in asking this right question, transformation can become
a reality for your church. To help your church ask and answer this right question, your Promised Land Task Force will invite people in your church to align
themselves to the vision and mission of discipleship for which Jesus prayed. In
sharing this invitation, your task force will model the vision and mission for
which Jesus prayed as you prepare and present a report on God's Promised
Land for Jesus' disciples. Modeling the characteristics of Christian transformation detailed in unit two, chapter four, your task force will connect the story
of your lives to the larger story of faith in Jesus, align the values of your lives

to Jesus' vision for life, and persevere in following Jesus. These characteristics
of Christian transformation are the desired outcome of your task force's ministry as you provide a strategic-ministry plan that will nurture and equip people faithfully to use the gifts God has given them.

The following structure and ministry responsibilities will provide the framework of
your Promised Land Task Force as you use the gifts God has given you. (You may
download an Action Plan Template of task-force responsibilities and a timeline at
www.upperroom.org/bookstore/prayer/ActionPlan.pdf.)

Promised Land Task-Force Chair: Primary responsibility is to guide
the task force in its work. This person should be a respected leader who is able
to hear, comprehend, and speak the languages of different concerns and voices
in your church. Respected as a person who is able to see your church objectively, the task-force chair will chair all meetings and be the primary
spokesperson of the task force.

Prayer Leader: Primary responsibility is to coordinate church-wide
prayer for the task force as it completes its responsibilities (i.e., worship services, church meetings, daily prayer guide, prayer vigil).

Communications Leader: Primary responsibility is to coordinate communications about the work of the task force through church publications
(i.e., bulletins, newsletter, emails, church web site, etc).

Small-Group Bible-Study Coordinator: Primary responsibility is to
recruit small-group Bible-study leaders who will lead the weekly studies and
facilitate discussion based on the three sets of questions found at the end of each
Bible study. The Small-Group Bible-Study Coordinator will emphasize to the
Bible-study leaders the intent of this Bible study to assist in the formation of a
strategic-ministry plan for your church. Bible-study leaders will accomplish this
as they facilitate responses to "Helping Your Voice to Be Heard" questions and
small-group dialogue. The coordinator will conduct a brief training session
reviewing the Bible-study leader's guide in the Participant's Workbook. At this
training session, the coordinator should emphasize the importance of Bible-
study leaders being neutral facilitators for discussion. The coordinator will also
want to review the process by which completed weekly "Helping Your Voice to
Be Heard" responses will be received by the coordinator.

The coordinator has responsibility for forwarding these responses to the
Data Coordinator.

Data Coordinator: Primary responsibility is to receive, assimilate, and
transmit data that will assist in the assessment of the current reality of your
church. Sources of data will include:

- Statistical information that reflects the three to five-year history of your church through worship attendance, participation in discipleship-formation classes, church membership, worship offerings, etc.

- Demographic information about your surrounding community such as population composition, surrounding churches, schools, etc. (An information tool to assist in the gathering of these statistical and demographic data is found online at www.upperroom.org/bookstore/prayer/StatsDemo.pdf and at www.faithfulljourney.org.)

- Small-group Bible-study responses gathered from the sets of questions entitled "Helping Your Voice to Be Heard." This data will be provided weekly by the Bible-study leaders as they collect responses from the participants in their Bible-study group. Each week, the Data Coordinator will combine all of the responses from the Bible-study groups using the form provided in Appendix 8. When all responses are compiled, a team selected by the task force will have the responsibility for interpreting the current reality of your church based on these responses. (Appendix 9 contains information about a resource tool that can assist in interpreting Bible-study responses. This tool, entitled The FaithFull Journey Current Reality Profile,^{SM} will provide a comprehensive, illustrative graphics presentation that will be unique to the Bible study responses of your church. A generic sample of this interpretive tool is located on the FaithFull Journey LLC* website at www.faithfulljourney.org.)

Mission Statement-Team Chair: Primary responsibility is to lead a Mission-Statement Team of five to seven people who will have the primary accountability for reviewing data and composing not less than three draft church-specific statements. The membership of the Mission-Statement Team should include members of the Promised Land Task Force and may include people from the church who are not members of the task force. The chair of the Mission-Statement Team should be a member of the Promised Land Task Force. Once the Mission-Statement Team forms, the Chair of the Mission-Statement Team and/or other people designated by the task force should review the key biblical concepts of the Bible studies. Chapter nine in this unit includes directions to assist the Mission-Statement Team in its work.

At-Large Members: The composition of your Promised Land Task Force should represent the different voices of your church. Although these people

---

*FaithFull Journey, LLC is owned and operated by the authors of *Does Your Church Have a Prayer* and is not affiliated with GBOD® or Discipleship Resources®.

may not have specific leadership tasks, their presence on the task force will assist in the consensus process. They may wish to lead one of the study groups, as this will give them a hands-on perspective.

Following the formation of the Promised Land Task Force for its assigned responsibilities, invite all people of your church to travel together through the journey of the strategic-ministry planning process. Broad-based participation by people in your church will enhance the discernment process as your church begins the journey of faith to God's Promised Land for Jesus' disciples. The Promised Land Task Force will want to extend an invitation through as many forms of communication as possible: worship services, discipleship groups, fellowship groups, newsletters, email communications, church web site, etc.

Send a letter of invitation to all members of the congregation telling of the support of the church's governing body for this season of spiritual engagement. In this letter, include the names of Promised Land Task Force members. Share the vision and mission of Jesus' prayer for his disciples. Encourage participation by people in your church as you let them know that their voice will be heard as they participate in a small-group Bible study and in public gatherings as the strategic-ministry plan is presented. Ask for their prayers and indication of support by signing a Covenant Card included in the letter you send.

The following is an example of a possible communication and Covenant Card that the pastor or key leaders may send to the congregation. (Appendix 4 includes a copy of the Strategic-Ministry Plan—Covenant Card along with other suggested communications.)

There is exciting news to share about our church! We are preparing to enter a process of spiritual engagement that will affect the future of our ministry and mission. Through a six-week Bible study series entitled *Does Your Church Have a Prayer? In Mission toward the Promised Land,* people in our congregation will gather in small Bible-study groups that will allow their voices to be heard. A strategic-ministry planning team (Promised Land Task Force) has formed to help our church discern how we can live in the reality of Jesus' prayer for our church. Members of this task force are (insert names).

Based on the understanding that Jesus' prayer for his disciples in John 17 includes the people who are part of our fellowship, we will consider how we can live into the reality of Jesus' prayer for our church. We invite you to allow your voice to be heard as you travel this journey of faith with your church through prayer, participation in a small study group, worship, and other times of gathering. If you would like your voice to be heard, please respond to this invitation by calling the church office.

We will organize our small groups based on availability and preferred times. A strategic-ministry plan—Covenant Card is included with this letter. As a symbol of your willingness to participate, please place it in the offering plate during our service of consecration on _____ or send to the Promised Land Task Force chairperson,_____. Will you join your friends in this time of personal renewal and congregational vision for our church?

Strategic-Ministry Plan

Covenant Card

John 17 includes Jesus' prayer for his followers. Our church will begin a process of study and listening that will help us to understand more fully how we can live in the vision and mission of Jesus' prayer. To assist in this process, a strategic-ministry plan team (the Promised Land Task Force) has been approved. Your support is important in helping the task force to hear the voice of our church through your prayers, participation in small-group Bible study, and listening session. As a sign of your support, return this Covenant Card to the church office.

Believing that Jesus has prayed for his followers, I will:

_____ Pray for the my church daily;

_____ Pray for the Promised Land Task Force;

_____ Allow my voice to be heard by participating in a small-group Bible study;

_____ Attend worship regularly;

_____ Participate in the listening session when the Promised Land Task Force presents its report.

_____ Signature

Task-force members who have responsibility for particular areas of emphasis will, in turn, coordinate and respond to people according to responses received.

As your task force fulfills its transforming responsibilities, you may wish to make the following prayer your covenant prayer as you witness to a story of faith that is bigger than your life, align the values of your life to Jesus' vision for life, and persevere as you lead by following Jesus:

> Holy God, you created us out of your love for humankind. It is out of your love for us that we have accepted your grace and chosen to follow Jesus, proclaiming the risen Christ. As Jesus' disciples, we know it is your desire for all the people of the world to be reconciled with you and one another for the redemption of all creation. We gather as your people now and give you thanks and praise for your presence in our lives. We give thanks for the ways in which you have guided and blessed this congregation. We too seek your will and guidance. Holy God, we gather to listen and discern together as we covenant to follow Jesus for your glory. Amen.

UNIT THREE

CHAPTER SEVEN

Starting the Journey

As a member of the Promised Land Task Force, you have the responsibility of helping your church to hear the invitation that God is placing before your congregation as you prepare to travel to the Promised Land for which Jesus prayed. This Promised Land for Jesus' disciples is not something your church will earn. It is an inheritance your church has been invited to receive as the risen Christ meets you. To live into this inheritance, people in your church must be willing to pull up stakes and become sojourners of faith. This will not be a simple journey. It will require your community of faith to face many questions and challenges as you make decisions that will call you to a land where you have never lived before. Consider this scripture:

> By faith Abraham obeyed when he was called to set out for a place that he was to receive as an inheritance; and he set out, not knowing where he was going. By faith he stayed for a time in the land he had been promised, as in a foreign land, living in tents, as did Isaac and Jacob, who were heirs with him of the same promise. For he looked forward to the city that has foundations, whose architect and builder is God. By faith he received power of procreation, even

though he was too old—and Sarah herself was barren—because he considered him faithful who had promised. Therefore from one person, and this one as good as dead, descendants were born, "as many as the stars of heaven and as the innumerable grains of sand by the seashore" (Hebrews 11:8-12).

God set before Abraham a vision and a mission. The vision was a land where Abraham had never lived before. The mission was a journey of faith Abraham had never traveled before. Obeying this vision and this mission, Abraham and his wife Sarah pulled up stakes from all they had ever known and became sojourners of faith. Living in tents, Abraham did not set down roots in this new land. Instead, Abraham's faith remained an active part of his life, always propelling him forward on the journey God had called him to travel. On this journey, Abraham and Sarah faced many questions. Bearing witness to the laughable challenges they faced was the name of their son Isaac, whose name means "laughter." A remarkable story of God's last laugh, the journey of the father and mother of faith is an invitation for all children of faith to travel a faithful journey that will lead to a Promised Land that contains no borders.

As your task force invites your church on this faithful journey, remember the remarkable story of God's last laugh through the cross of Jesus as told in 1 Corinthians 1:18: "For the message about the cross is foolishness to those who are perishing, but to us who are being saved it is the power of God." In preparing for this journey, you will want to enlist the key leadership of your church for their blessing. Inviting them to travel to God's Promised Land for Jesus' disciples, you will follow the example of Abraham and Sarah in Genesis 12:4-5 who left nothing behind as they set out on their journey to the land God promised them:

> So Abram went, as the LORD had told him; and Lot went with him. Abram was seventy-five years old when he departed from Haran. Abram took his wife Sarai and his brother's son Lot, and all the possessions that they had gathered, and the people whom they had acquired in Haran; and they set forth to go to the land of Canaan.

The key leaders you will invite to travel this journey with you are your church's governing body. It is important not to leave them behind as you set out on this journey. When there are staff members in a church, your lead pastor will be the person who invites them to participate in this ministry planning process. Members of your church's staff have the ability to interpret this venture as a blessing for your church in ways that are positive. They also have the ability to raise questions in ways that are negative and may undermine the whole strategic-ministry planning process. Your lead pastor will teach your church staff the foundational understandings, key concepts, and key scriptural points of the Bible studies so that the staff may respond with confidence when others ask them about the intent of this planning process. Church staff should also sign the same commitment cards that your Advance Leadership Team and Promised Land Task Force leadership have signed as an indication of their support.

To answer questions that may arise within the congregation about the objectivity of the planning process, it is important that church staff should not be members of the task force. In many churches, members of church staff represent the voices of different concerns that may not want to change direction as the church enters the reality Jesus envisioned for his followers. For the protection of the church staff and the validity of the strategic-ministry plan that is developed, do not involve church staff in the decision making process of the Promised Land Task Force.

In consultation with your pastor, your Advance Leadership Team will be responsible for interpreting the strategic-ministry planning process to your church's governing body in ways that invite them into dialogue that builds your community of faith. As your team interprets this process, your governing body will learn that *Does Your Church Have a Prayer? In Mission toward the Promised Land* is built on Jesus' prayer for his disciples in John 17. Have copies of the Participant's Workbook available for members of your governing body to review.

As you present the strategic-ministry planning process, you may face questions as you invite your church to make decisions that will call it to God's Promised Land for Jesus' disciples. Respond to these questions by telling of the inheritance that your church has been invited to receive as you live in Jesus' vision of **living in joy and unity in Jesus to the glory of God** and the mission of being **followers of Jesus sent into the world**. Ask questions that invite open and healthy dialogue within your governing body. Beginning this journey, remember that God has the last laugh as you model the traits of transformational leadership: remembering encouragement, ability to ask the right questions, ability to see beyond self-focused concerns, and lead by the redeemed need to serve.

Asking faithful questions that offer a hope-filled vision of the future, seek the commitment of these people to the strategic planning process through their prayers, participation in small Bible-study groups, and other related activities. Tell them how this process of strategic-ministry planning is a time of spiritual engagement as your church engages in a Bible-study series that will facilitate congregational feedback. Have your pastor tell of her or his enthusiastic support for this process. Present the names of the Promised Land Task Force your team and/or church nominating committee is recommending for approval by the governing body. (If additional people are added to the task force by the governing body, consult with them about the expectations of their commitment as the task force begins its work.)

As you present this process to your governing body, ask the members to indicate their support by completing and returning the same covenant card you have signed. This will indicate their commitment to the strategic-ministry planning process. Moving forward in the journey before you, it is important that you have these signs of commitment in case questions arise later regarding the support of your church's leadership. (A reproducible copy of this Strategic-Ministry Plan—Covenant Card is included in Appendix 4.) At the conclusion of your presentation, invite them to join your leadership team in the covenant prayer that your church will use in the strategic-ministry planning process:

> Holy God, you created us out of your love for humankind. It is out of your love for us that we have accepted your grace and chosen to follow Jesus, proclaiming the risen Christ. As Jesus' disciples, we know it is your desire for all the people of the world to be reconciled with you and one another for the redemption of all creation.
>
> We gather as your people now and give you thanks and praise for your presence in our lives. We give thanks for the ways in which you have guided and blessed this congregation. We too seek your will and guidance. Holy God, we gather to listen and discern together as we covenant to follow Jesus for your glory. Amen.

UNIT THREE

CHAPTER EIGHT

Assessing Current Reality

Your Promised Land Task Force has the responsibility of helping your church to develop a strategic-ministry plan that is built on a solid foundation of the present. To ask future-tense questions about your envisioned reality, your Promised Land Task Force must first answer present-tense questions about your current reality. Your faithful answers to these present-tense questions will provide a solid foundation as your congregation faces the challenges of the future. Consider these words from scripture:

> "Everyone then who hears these words of mine and acts on them will be like a wise man who built his house on rock. The rain fell, the floods came, and the winds blew and beat on that house, but it did not fall, because it had been founded on rock. And everyone who hears these words of mine and does not act on them will be like a foolish man who built his house on sand. The rain fell, and the floods came, and the winds blew and beat against that house, and it fell—and great was its fall!" (Matthew 7:24-27).

Jesus told his disciples a parable about the present so that he could teach them a lesson about the future. Foundational to Jesus' lesson about the future was the importance of assessing current reality. Teaching that the results of future reality are built on the foundation of current reality, Jesus talked about the difference between building on rock and sand.

Through the accompanying small-group Bible-study guide (Participant's Workbook), your church's leadership team will invite your congregation into a time of reflection and conversation about the future as you assess the foundation of current reality. The strategic-ministry planning process that you will be using has a distinctive approach for assessing the current reality of your church. Rather than assessing your church's current reality through the reflections of a small group of people, your Promised Land Task Force will assess the current reality of your church through a process of spiritual engagement that will help the broad-based voice of your congregation to be heard.

As your church engages in small-group studies, responses recorded each week to questions found in a section entitled "Helping Your Voice to Be Heard" will reflect the "voice of many." The answers of your small-group Bible-study participants provides will present a snapshot of the current reality of your church. You may choose to develop your own internal assessment of this snapshot of your church's current reality, or you may receive a Current Reality Profile[SM] provided by FaithFull Journey, LLC as detailed in Appendix 9.

In order for the church to receive your strategic-ministry plan as an envisioned and valid plan for the future, it must reflect an objective and valid report of the present reality of your congregation. This honest assessment is part of the vital leadership role your Promised Land Task Force will provide.

To assist you in your leadership responsibility of developing a strategic-ministry plan that the church will receive as a valid discernment of its collective voice, you will incorporate biblical concepts that your small-group Bible-study participants will be learning and that your pastor will be preaching about. In doing this, your eventual strategic planning report will be based on the same principles that the congregation has learned and with which they can resonate as their voices are heard through the plan you present. The following Bible studies contain these biblical concepts. The explanations for each concept also contain suggestions for how your team may assess the current reality of your church.

Bible Study Three

The Language of Your Church

Bible study three identifies two types of languages that are spoken in a church: the language of remembering encouragement and the language of murmuring.

The language of remembering encouragement remembers the past faithfulness of God and encourages members of a church to live into the promise of God's future faithfulness. Disciples of Jesus Christ are called to focus their faith on God's faithfulness as revealed through Jesus. Joshua and Caleb spoke the language of remembering encouragement as they interpreted the challenges of the present through a God-sized vision of the future. Encouraging remembrance is the language of envisioned reality.

The language of murmuring describes life in congregations that allow fears of the present and future to combine with a desire to cling to the past. Murmuring was the language of the congregation of Israel as they faced the challenges of the wilderness and the Promised Land. The topic of murmuring is often disappointment with the perception of a church's present ministry and a tendency to focus more on fear of the future than hope for the future. In the vocabulary of murmuring, the past tense is heard more often than the future tense. Murmuring is the language of perceived reality.

Begin to listen to the type of language people speak in your church. Give attention to the phrases that people use; listen to see if the future tense or the past tense defines the language of your congregation. Be sensitive to whether fear of the future or hope for the future defines your congregation. You may find it helpful to keep a list of the words and phrases that you hear as you determine if the language is one of envisioned reality or the language of perceived reality.

Naming the Giants

All Promised Lands have giants dwelling in them. Bible study three identifies some giants that are general in nature to the total church: worldviews, technology, and expectations. This Bible study also invites participants to identify the giants that are specific to your congregation and that may be hindering your church from entering the Promised Land Jesus envisioned for his disciples in John 17. In order to overcome general and specific giants, a congregation must allow its vision to focus beyond the fearful reality of giants. This will happen only as the congregation focuses on living as people sent into the world through the power of God's love. Members of congregations may respond to the challenges facing them by focusing their vision on the promise of God's faithfulness. They may also respond to the challenge of the giants by focusing their vision upon themselves. Every congregation must make conscious choices about how it will deal with the general and specific giants it is facing.

What are the current challenges you face as a church? Are there congregational or neighborhood demographics, financial challenges, an aging facility, changes in the number of church members, changes in worship attendance, a history of conflict, etc., that you would identify as giants? Are there specific giants in your church that have taken on mythical proportions as they shape and control the culture and structure of your church? Do the specific giants your church faces cause members to focus within their own concerns about institutional survival rather than looking beyond themselves as missional expressions of God's Holy Spirit? Is your church controlled by fears of the giants it faces or by hope and remembering encouragement of God's promised faithfulness?

Bible Study Four

Asking the Right Questions

As people of faith in Jesus Christ, we must listen carefully and understand the questions we are asking as well as the questions other people are asking. Right questions lead to faithful conversation that builds the life of the community because they help us to say who we think Jesus is. Wrong questions discredit people with whom we disagree. Our intent and the intent of other people reside in the questions that we ask.

What are the questions you are hearing in your church? What are the traditional questions that you have heard? Is there one specific question that voices ask in your church or about your church? Does your church have questions about its future? What are the questions people ask when the governing body meets? What are the questions people ask in the church parking lot, through emails, and through other means of communication in your church? Do questions in your church usually invite dialogue from diverse opinions? Do questions in your church discredit dialogue from diverse opinions? What is an example of a wrong question in your church? What is an example of a right question in your church?

What Were You Discussing on the Way?

Every congregation needs to have an understanding of its history and how it arrived at its current reality. "What were you discussing on the way" is the question Jesus asked his disciples when they engaged in a power struggle over who was the greatest among them. Jesus asked this question to invite his disciples to assess the current reality of their discipleship. It is the question that congregations need to answer as they assess their current reality and live into envisioned reality.

Does the history of your church reflect repeated power struggles? Are there repeated discussions in your church about what your congregation values most? Instead of making statements about who is right and who is wrong, does your church's leadership talk about what it means to have faith in the Savior who was last of all and servant of all? Instead of making statements about who is right and who is wrong, is there potential for your congregation to begin asking where to find God's true power when Jesus is confessed as Christ?

Bible Study Five

Beyond and Within

This scripture describes the biblical concept of *Beyond and Within*:
> He called the crowd with his disciples, and said to them, "If any want to become my followers, let them deny themselves and take up their cross and follow me. For those who want to save their life will lose it, and those who lose their life for my sake, and for the sake of the gospel, will save it. For what will it profit them to gain the whole world and forfeit their life? Indeed, what can they give in return for their life?" (Mark 8:34-37).

Beyond and Within teaches that the current reality of discipleship is always assessed through the transforming truth of the cross of Jesus. This invitation to discipleship mandates that the vision of discipleship must be beyond self-focused concerns as Jesus' followers take up their cross and lose their lives for Jesus' sake and the gospel's. The goal for ministry within these congregations is that they empower people to live as Jesus' disciples and transform the present values of their lives for Jesus' sake and the gospel's.

Churches that apply this biblical teaching assess the current reality of their ministry by how they are inviting people to be disciples of Jesus as they see beyond their self-focused concerns. Remembering Jesus' admonition to lose their lives for his sake and the gospel's, they share the love of God by focusing beyond their own concerns. Through this same self-giving vision, they also look within at those things that are hindering them from living as God's called people. Following Jesus' sacrificial example of love, the cross of Jesus transforms them.

Does the principle of *Beyond and Within* define the current reality of your church? How does your church's current ministry invite people to be followers of Jesus as they see beyond their self-focused concerns? Does your church look within at those things that are hindering your members from living as God's called people?

Bible Study Six

The Mind of Christ

Transformed congregations recognize that complacency with past success will likely cause their ministry to plateau and ultimately begin a stage of decline. Transformational leaders and members create new expressions of ministry that define the mind of Christ among them (found in Philippians 2:5-11). Being proactive in achieving congregational consensus, they understand that all organizations go through life cycles. Acknowledging cherished memories of the past and cherished ministries of the present, these congregations are able to respect what gives foundation to the present reality of their faith. While these memories and ministries are respected, they are not to be worshiped. Doing so precludes the ability to focus beyond the present into God's envisioned reality. Looking beyond their own interests, transformational congregations make intentional choices that help them to grow in their mission of witnessing to the grace of God in Jesus Christ.

Does your congregation have a history of honestly assessing its current reality? Does your church make intentional decisions about its ministry and mission? Are there certain characteristics about your church that need to be changed in order for it to grow in its mission of witnessing to the grace of God in Jesus Christ? Are there new expressions of ministry in your church or included in its planning?

Identifying the Tribes of Your Congregation

In addition to receiving your congregation's feedback from the Bible studies, your leadership team will need to identify the different concerns or tribes that form the current composition of your congregation. Just as the congregation of Israel had twelve tribes that composed it, today's churches have different voices that are heard in their communities of faith. While the Participant's Workbook addresses the reality of different concerns that are found in a congregation, it does not invite participants to identify or name the specific tribes that form your congregation. Identifying the specific tribes that form your congregation is the responsibility of your leadership team.

As you discern, prepare, and present your church's strategic-ministry plan, you will want to be aware of the different voices in your church. These voices, or tribes, have the power to endorse or voice opposition to your plan. It is essential that various tribes know they have either been heard or been given the opportunity to be heard in the planning process. This allows the total congregation to acknowledge your leadership team as a fair and objective voice even though the plan it presents may offer a vision that is different from the one currently voiced in your church. The following tribes or voices may be heard in many churches. Your team may also identify other tribes or voices that are heard in the context of your church's life.

The Tribe of the Good Old Days

This tribe is primarily concerned with memory preservation of the perceived past glory days of a congregation. It sees the church as a place that harbors the security of past memories in the midst of a changing world. While this tribe is not opposed to new people in the church, it is understood that these new people's primary role is to support the church's present ministry structure and not to rock the boat. We hear the voice of this tribe through such questions and statements as: "What's wrong with the way we're doing things now?" "I remember when our pews used to be filled and our Sunday school rooms were overflowing with children"; "Why can't we do things like we used to?"; You're sitting in my pew."

The Tribe of Forgetting the Past

This tribe is primarily concerned with living into the future without understanding how the history of a church affects its present and future ministry. This tribe understands tradition as a roadblock to the future. Its members cherish their roles of rocking the boat. The voice of this tribe is heard through such questions and statements as: "The past is the past. Let's move on"; "Times have changed"; "You're too old"; "You don't get it"; "Why do we have to spend so much time talking about the past?"

The Tribe of Control

This tribe is primarily concerned with power. Members of this tribe believe that they are responsible for running the church. Within this tribe, preservation of control is a primary concern, even though the language of this tribe is cloaked in words of concern for the overall life of the church. This tribe sees its role as preserving the church for future generations, often at the expense of the present generation. The voice of this tribe is heard through such questions and statements as: "I am responsible for this ministry"; "This is my job;"

"You don't understand"; "I'm withholding my giving"; "I'm designating my giving"; "Now is not the time"; "If anyone else would like to do this job, I'd be glad to give it up"; "What do you mean, give up my job?"

The Tribe of Spiritual Elitism

This tribe is concerned with judging the spiritual vitality of a congregation by its own values of faith. Members of this tribe are defined by their adherence to specific doctrinal beliefs that give security to their lives or by personal experiences that give validity to their expressions of faith. This tribe believes it is responsible for determining the credibility of other people's leadership by its self-imposed standards of spirituality. The voice of this tribe is heard through such questions and statements as: "You'll understand one day"; "God will make it clear to you"; "This is what the Bible means"; "I'm right, you're wrong"; "What do you mean, I might be wrong?"

The Tribe of Business Values

This tribe is concerned with judging the vitality of a church by its own values of business life. Members of this tribe are defined by their adherence to specific business practices that give security to their businesses. This tribe believes the church must be run like a business if it is going to survive. The voice of this tribe is heard through such questions and statements as: "Faith doesn't balance budgets"; "We need to run the church like a business"; "What's the bottom line?"

The Tribe of Apathy

This tribe is concerned with giving the appearance of not being concerned. Members of this tribe care about the church, but they have detached themselves from voicing an opinion because they realize they are not valued by other tribes within the church. This tribe believes the church can survive with them or without them. The voice of this tribe is heard through such questions and statements as: "Whatever"; "Don't ask me"; "I don't care"; "Don't bother me"; "Leave me alone"; "Do you really want to know?"

The Tribe of Remembering Encouragers

This tribe is concerned with helping the congregation to live into the envisioned reality for which Jesus prayed. Members of this tribe care about the church, understand the importance of faithful remembering, and persist in their faith. This tribe believes the church exists for one reason: to glorify God. The voice of this tribe is heard through such questions and statements as: "I hear what you are saying"; "God is with us"; "I really want to know"; "Why haven't we done it that way before?"; "Where is God calling us as a community of faith?"; "How we can move forward together?"

Some or all of these tribes may be present in your church. Some of these tribes may have been present for generations. Other tribes may be more recent. In assessing the current reality of your church, you must be aware of the voices of each tribe as you answer questions about your community of faith. As you develop your church's strategic-ministry plan, you will want to determine how your team will address the present concerns of these tribes so that they may hear together the voice of God.

Gathering Other Assessment Information

As your Promised Land Task Force assimilates the responses from Bible study participants and from your own observation of the tribes or voices in your church, collect data about the current reality of your church that will assist you in your discernment of your strategic-ministry plan. This data should include the following statistical information that reflects the past three to five-year history of your church: worship attendance, attendance in educational or discipleship classes, church membership, worship offerings, special offerings, mission groups, etc. Your task force will also want to gather demographic information about your surrounding community: population composition, surrounding churches, schools, businesses, etc. This information will provide essential background information as your task force considers future implications and suggestions for your church's ministry and mission focus. (Download tools to help collect this data at www.upperroom.org/bookstore/prayer/ChurchStats.pdf, www.upperroom.org/bookstore/prayer/StatsDemo.pdf, or at www.faithfulljourney.org.)

The importance of accurately assessing the current reality of your church cannot be overstated. For your congregation to withstand the challenges of the future, it must give careful attention to the development of a comprehensive strategy that is based on an objective assessment of your church's current reality. Remembering Jesus' parable about the difference between building on rock and sand, it is essential that you discern how the current reality of your church can provide a firm foundation for the future. As your Promised Land Task Force is faithful to this responsibility, you will lead your church to hear the words of Jesus and act on them.

UNIT THREE

CHAPTER NINE

Developing a Strategic-Ministry Plan

Your church can live in the envisioned reality for which Jesus prayed. Entering God's Promised Land for Jesus' disciples, your community of faith must build on the vision of living in joy and unity in Jesus to the glory of God and the mission of being followers of Jesus sent into the world. The development of a strategic-ministry plan will help your congregation align itself to the reality for which Jesus prayed as your church makes strategic choices about its nature and mission so the world may know that God sent Jesus. Recall Jesus as he prayed:

> "The glory that you have given me I have given them, so that they may be one, as we are one, I in them and you in me, that they may become completely one, so that the world may know that you have sent me and have loved them even as you have loved me" (John 17:22-23).

Jesus prayed that his disciples would make intentional choices that would allow them to follow him. Envisioning a reality where his followers become fishers of people by becoming the least of all and the servants of all, Jesus prayed. Envisioning a reality where his followers bear their crosses as they

80

deny themselves for his sake and for the sake of the gospel, Jesus prayed. Envisioning a Promised Land where his followers would live in joy and unity glorifying God as they live in the glory Jesus has given them, Jesus prayed.

Like the congregation of Israel, your congregation will need to receive a report about the Promised Land. Your report will indicate the degree to which your church lives into the reality Jesus has envisioned for your church. In turn, you must choose if you wish to enter that Promised Land. Like the congregation of Israel, your congregation will need to decide if it wishes to face the giants that dwell in the reality Jesus has envisioned or wander in search of a meaning for its existence.

Your Promised Land Task Force has been entrusted with the responsibility of presenting a faithful report to your congregation. It will present this report in the form of a strategic-ministry plan shaped by the biblical principles of the small-group Bible studies that your church will be participating in and that your pastor will preach about through a six-week sermon series. Alignment of your congregation to the envisioned reality for which Jesus prayed will occur as participants and worshipers become familiar with and discuss the foundational understandings, key concepts, and key scriptural points on which your strategic-ministry plan is based.

Using the ministry assessment model outlined in Acts 6:1-7 of Bible study five, your Promised Land Task Force will define the mission of the congregation, assess your congregation's current reality through mission values, organize a response through consultation with leadership, and achieve consensus by the congregation. This model will enable your congregation's current reality to be transformed by unity of vision and consensus of mission.

Aligning Your Church with Jesus' Vision and Mission

Following is a model for your task force to use as you develop your strategic-ministry plan. In addition, download the Step-by-Step Task Force Facilitation Guide at www.upperroom.org/bookstore/prayer/TaskFroce.pdf or at www.faithfulljourney.org. These tools can assist your task force with a schedule of specific roles and tasks.

Step 1: Align Your Church with Jesus' Vision

The Envisioned Reality for Which Jesus Prayed

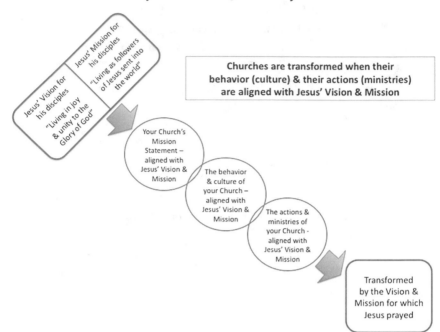

The Current Reality of Many Churches

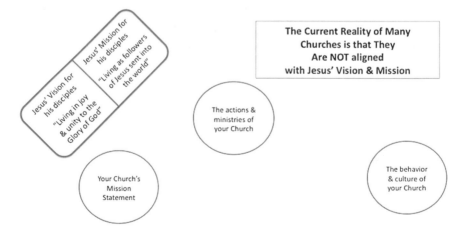

Steps toward Alignment

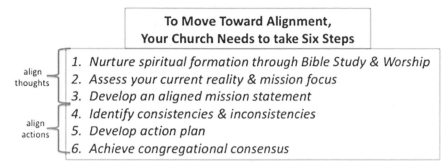

**To Move Toward Alignment,
Your Church Needs to take Six Steps**

align
thoughts

1. *Nurture spiritual formation through Bible Study & Worship*
2. *Assess your current reality & mission focus*
3. *Develop an aligned mission statement*

align
actions

4. *Identify consistencies & inconsistencies*
5. *Develop action plan*
6. *Achieve congregational consensus*

Step 1: Nurture Spiritual Formation through Bible Study and Worship

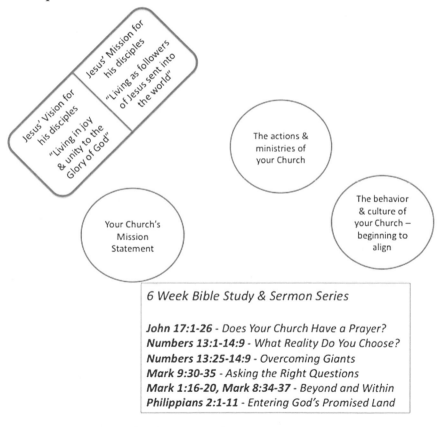

Jesus' Mission for his disciples "Living as followers of Jesus sent into the world"

Jesus' Vision for his disciples "Living in joy & unity to the Glory of God"

The actions & ministries of your Church

The behavior & culture of your Church — beginning to align

Your Church's Mission Statement

6 Week Bible Study & Sermon Series

John 17:1-26 - Does Your Church Have a Prayer?
Numbers 13:1-14:9 - What Reality Do You Choose?
Numbers 13:25-14:9 - Overcoming Giants
Mark 9:30-35 - Asking the Right Questions
Mark 1:16-20, Mark 8:34-37 - Beyond and Within
Philippians 2:1-11 - Entering God's Promised Land

Jesus established the vision and mission for all churches in his prayer in John 17. As the members of your congregation work through the Bible studies, they should become familiar with and embrace these tenets:

- Vision for your church, "Joy and Unity in Jesus to the Glory of God";
- Mission for your church, "Followers of Jesus Sent into the World."

Through acts of faithfulness that point beyond their own concerns, churches can align themselves with the vision of Jesus' prayer in John 17. Guided by the biblical principle of *Beyond and Within*, communities of faith can be defined by Jesus' vision and mission for his disciples. As your Promised Land Task Force prepares its report, you will need to ask right questions about your church's alignment with Jesus' vision. Some of these right questions are: "Does joy define our church?"; "Is our church united in our vision?"; "Is our church's vision united in our ministries?"; "When people look at our church, do they see a congregation that is a symbol of joy and unity in Jesus to the glory of God?"; "Can our church's mission be defined as being followers of Jesus sent into the world?" If your answer to these questions is *yes*, then your report will need to affirm the ways your church is currently aligned to Jesus' vision and mission for his disciples. If your answer to these questions is *no*, then your report will need to identify the giants or challenges that your church must overcome in order for it to align itself to Jesus' envisioned reality. For most congregations, the answers to these right questions will be both *yes* and *no*. There will be some areas of congregational life that are aligned with Jesus' vision, and there will be some areas of congregational life that are not aligned with Jesus' vision.

God calls all churches to align themselves with the vision and mission of Jesus' prayer. The vision of joy and unity in Jesus to the glory of God is the vision that guides every church as it lives in the reality of Jesus' prayer for his disciples. While there are many different contexts in which local churches find themselves, the common foundation that all churches share is Jesus' prayer for them. When communities of Jesus' disciples are willing to align themselves to the envisioned reality of Jesus' prayer, transformation occurs. Step 1 (a six-week, small-group Bible study and worship sermon series) provides the foundation for the entire strategic-ministry planning process. It is the premise of this foundational first step that churches can live into a future that is different from their past. Building on the understanding that faith in Jesus transforms hearts and minds, communities of Jesus' disciples can be transformed as they align themselves to the vision and mission of Jesus' prayer through study and worship together.

Step 2: Assess Your Church's Current Reality and Mission Focus

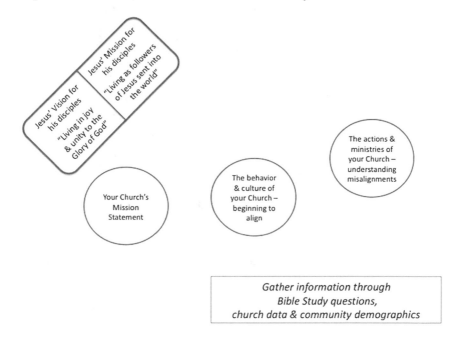

A broad-based assessment of your church's current reality is essential in developing a strategic-ministry plan that will faithfully align your congregation to the vision and mission for which Jesus prayed. Having a clear and accurate understanding of where your church currently finds itself will enable your task force to develop a roadmap for the future that acknowledges the challenges and strengths of the present. There are two elements important to understanding your church's current reality.

1. Church and Community Data

Gather data about the recent three to five years of the history of your church as highlighted in chapter eight of unit three, including worship attendance, attendance in educational or discipleship classes, church membership, worship offerings, special offerings, mission groups, etc. Your Promised Land Task Force will also want to gather demographic information about your surrounding community, including population composition, surrounding churches, schools, businesses, etc. Your Promised Land Task Force should gather this data prior to the conclu-

sion of the Bible studies. (Download data information tools at
www.upperroom.org/bookstore/prayer/ChurchStats.pdf,
www.upperroom.org/bookstore/prayer/StatsDemo.pdf or at
www.faithfulljourney.org.)

2. "Helping Your Voice to Be Heard" Responses

Compile, sort, and analyze responses from the "Helping Your Voice to
Be Heard" questions in Bible study participants that will provide a
broad-based understanding of the current culture of your church. It is
important to include the giants that are identified from the responses
as you compile, sort, and analyze the responses.

As your task force gathers and analyzes the data, allow the data to speak objectively for itself. It is important for your task force's report of your church's current reality to be received as an objective assessment by the different voices that
form your congregation. FaithFull Journey, LLC can provide a custom analysis
for your individual church. It includes a presentation of both the Church and
Community Data and "Helping Your Voice to Be Heard" responses. Information
about this Current Reality Profile^{SM} analysis tool is available in Appendix 9.

Your task force will also need to assess the challenges or giants that are facing your church. Detailed in Bible study three, two types of giants face a congregation. There are general giants such as differing worldviews, technology,
and expectations. In addition, there are also giants that are specific to the context in which a church finds itself: behavior patterns, attendance, finances, vol-
unteers, etc. It is essential that your assessment acknowledge the challenges
that your church is facing as it seeks to live into the reality Jesus envisioned for
his disciples. In acknowledging these giants, it is also essential that your strategic-
ministry plan focus on the promise of God's faithfulness that will empower you
to overcome the giants. While giants present challenges for a congregation,
they also offer a great occasion for a local church to help people understand
there is a God who cares about them in ways that are relevant to the present
challenges of life.

Step 3: Develop an Aligned Mission Statement

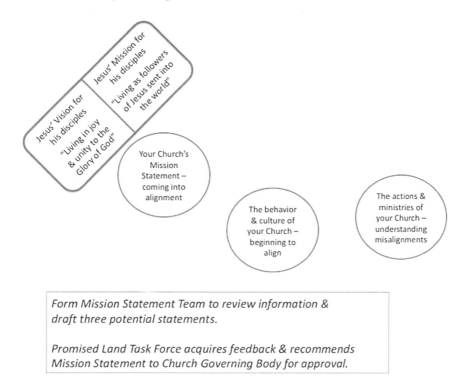

In preparing for the writing of the strategic-ministry plan, the task force will need to agree that the desired outcome of this strategic ministry process is to align the vision and mission of your church with the vision and mission of Jesus' prayer for his disciples. Throughout the discernment process, the Promised Land Task Force must filter its work through the vision of living in joy and unity in Jesus to the glory of God and the mission of being followers of Jesus sent into the world. This vision and mission will guide your development of a mission statement specific to your church. If your church already has a mission statement, then you should assess your current mission statement through Jesus' prayer.

A significant part of your work as a Promised Land Task Force will be the development of a mission statement that aligns itself to the vision and mission of Jesus' prayer through your church's context of ministry.

Although many churches find mission-statement development intimidating, a simple process to assist your task force is outlined in the following:

1. Once the six-week Bible study is completed and data is compiled, the Promised Land Task Force forms a small team of five to seven people to serve as the Mission-Statement Team.
2. Mission-Statement Team Chair and/or other people designated by the Promised Land Task Force review key biblical concept of *Beyond and Within* with the Mission-Statement Team.
3. Mission-Statement Team brainstorms completion of the following statement, "Our church can glorify God by. . . ."
4. Mission-Statement Team reviews data and composes three draft statements for consideration by the Promised Land Task Force and church's governing body.

As noted above, the Promised Land Task Force should form a Mission-Statement Team that will have the primary accountability for reviewing data and composing three drafts of your church-specific mission statements. Membership of the Mission-Statement Team should include members of the task force and may include people from the church who are not members of the task force. A member of the Promised Land Task Force should be the chairperson of the Mission-Statement Team. Once the Mission-Statement Team forms, the chairperson of the Mission-Statement Team should review the key biblical concept of *Beyond and Within*. Members of the Mission-Statement Team must agree that the desired outcome of this strategic ministry process is to align the vision and mission of your church with the vision and mission of Jesus' prayer for his disciples. Only then can the Mission-Statement Team interpret the data from the ministry-planning package and draft statements that are in alignment with Jesus' envisioned reality for your church.

The biblical principle of *Beyond and Within* should guide the development of a mission statement or the review of your church's current mission statement. Detailed in Bible study five, this principle calls a congregation to look beyond itself as it understands its reason for existence. The goal of your mission statement and resultant plan is to develop a vision that will align life within your congregation to the reason for its existence: the mission of living as Jesus' followers sent into the world. To achieve this goal, your strategic-ministry plan must have a mission statement specifically developed for the current reality in which your church finds itself.

In preparing its drafts of potential mission statements, begin by brainstorming the completion of the statement, "Our church can glorify God by. . . ." The team should then review available data as provided by the Data Coordinator.

You may include your church's current mission statement (if applicable) with the drafts of potential mission statements. Potential mission drafts should be no longer than two sentences and should succinctly state the desired reality of how your church nurtures and equips people to be followers of Jesus sent into the world.

After potential mission drafts are written, they are to be presented to your Promised Land Task Force and then to your church's governing body in a public forum that invites the entire church to attend. The intent of this public forum is to receive feedback that will assist the task force in recommending a church mission statement to the governing body for adjustment and ultimate approval.

Step 4: Identify Consistencies and Inconsistencies

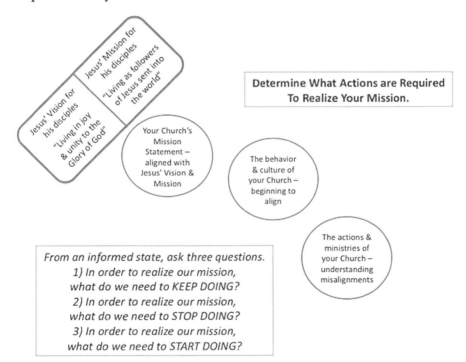

Steps 1 through 3 have helped to define clearly the alignment of your church's mission statement with the envisioned reality for which Jesus prayed. You also have objective information regarding your church's current reality. The time has now come to make decisions regarding the ways in which your church's current reality is consistent or inconsistent with your church's mission statement.

One demonstrated means of generating this information is for your Promised Land Task Force to answer the following questions about your church's current reality:

> **Keep Doing:** In order to move toward Jesus' envisioned reality for our church, what do we need to maintain in our current reality?
>
> **Stop Doing:** In order to move toward Jesus' envisioned reality for our church, what do we need to retire in our current reality?
>
> **Start Doing:** In order to move toward Jesus' envisioned reality for our church, what do we need to create?

The identification of consistencies and inconsistencies with recommended goals will naturally sort into two dimensions of desired outcomes:

1. The first dimension focuses on **relationship**. This dimension emphasizes ministries of your church that nurture followers of Jesus to live in joy and unity to the glory of God.

2. The second dimension focuses on **task**. This dimension emphasizes ministries of your church that equip followers of Jesus to be sent into the world.

A desired outcome is more than the setting of a ministry goal. It is a foundational understanding of the reason your plan recommends a specific ministry goal. As your team writes the strategic-ministry plan, remember that the desired outcome of your plan is to invite your church to live in the envisioned reality for which Jesus prayed. Philippians 2:1-4, as found in Bible study six, reflects the desired outcome for which Jesus prayed:

> If then there is any encouragement in Christ, any consolation from love, any sharing in the Spirit, any compassion and sympathy, make my joy complete: be of the same mind, having the same love, being in full accord and of one mind. Do nothing from selfish ambition or conceit, but in humility regard others as better than yourselves. Let each of you look not to your own interests, but to the interests of others.

Your plan should include ministry goals that encourage people in your church to nurture each other as a community of faith through joy and unity in Jesus to the glory of God. As you establish desired outcomes for nurturing ministries in your plan, affirm areas of your church's current ministry that are consistent with the behaviors that Paul's letter to the Philippians advocates. Using Paul's words, allow your report to be an encouragement in Christ as you look not to your own interests but to the interests of others. Without accusation or judgment, your plan should be an objective assessment of the current reality of your church. It should present ministry goals that will nurture people in your community of faith to live in a Promised Land of discipleship defined by Philippians 2:1-4.

Your strategic-ministry plan should also include ministry goals that equip people in your church to live as followers of Jesus sent into the world. Philippians 2:5-11, as found in Bible study six, reflects the desired outcome of ministries in your church that equip people to be doers of the word:

> Let the same mind be in you that was in Christ Jesus, who, though he was in the form of God, did not regard equality with God as something to be exploited, but emptied himself, taking the form of a slave, being born in human likeness. And being found in human form, he humbled himself and became obedient to the point of death—even death on a cross. Therefore God also highly exalted him and gave him the name that is above every name, so that at the name of Jesus every knee should bend, in heaven and on earth and under the earth, and every tongue should confess that Jesus Christ is Lord, to the glory of God the Father.

As you establish desired outcomes for equipping ministries in your plan, affirm current ministries that are helping people in your church to have the mind of Christ in them. Guided by the biblical principle of *Beyond and Within*, your plan should acknowledge areas of consistency and inconsistency with the desired mission of Jesus' prayer. As highlighted in Bible study four, your plan should invite your church to consider where true power is found in the lives of Jesus' followers as they seek to be last of all and servants of all.

In discerning a strategic-ministry plan, your Promised Land Task Force must be faithful to the four traits of leadership considered in your selection. These four traits of leadership are remembering encouragement, ability to ask the right questions, ability to see beyond self-focused concerns, and leading by the redeemed need to serve. These leadership qualities, highlighted in unit three, chapter six, will form the criteria for your task force's self-assessment as you write your church's strategic-ministry plan. Throughout the process of discernment, your task force should judge the effectiveness of your written plan by how it invites your congregation to exhibit these same traits of leadership through its ministry.

The authors will need to consult with the Promised Land Task Force for feedback as they prepare the plan. They may do this as they complete the plan or wait until they write it in its entirety. Following the completion of the written plan, the task force will engage in holy conversation as it considers the plan as a whole document and determines if it faithfully invites your congregation to align itself to the reality for which Jesus prayed.

Bible study six includes a biblical example of how your task force may engage in this holy conversation. It is the story of the Jerusalem Council in Acts 15, when Jewish and Gentile Christians looked beyond their self-focused concerns to the larger vision and mission of being disciples of Jesus. In order to achieve this vision and mission, both Jewish and Gentile Christians agreed to set aside those things that hindered them from looking to the interests of others, to continue those things that gave foundation to their faith, and to create new expressions of ministry and mission. Following the model of the Jerusalem Council, your strategic-ministry plan will give your congregation the opportunity to look to the larger vision and mission of being disciples of Jesus. It will present goals that will require intentional choices about the present and future ministries of your church. Each goal that your plan presents should be based on a desired outcome that invites your church to consider which ministries it needs to keep, start, or stop.

Step 5: Develop Action Plan

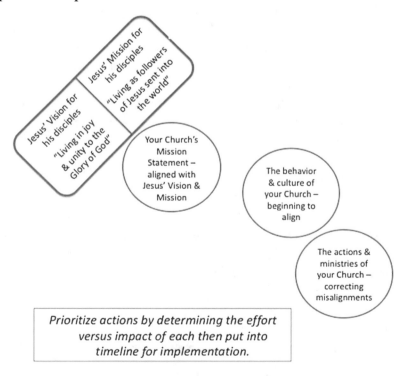

Your task force's ministry plan must acknowledge how God's faithfulness has been and is being experienced in your church. It, however, must not dwell in the past or the present. Rather than protecting cherished memories of the past or cherished ministries of the present, your plan must focus on how your church may share the gospel of Jesus Christ in the current reality of its ministry. The strategic-ministry plan that your group discerns must be an invitation for your church to align its vision and mission to a journey of discipleship that leads beyond the past and present contexts of its ministry. In order to extend this invitation, your task force needs to develop a strategic-ministry plan that asks the right questions of your church.

Approach Is Important to Outcome

As the authors write the ministry plan, it is essential that your questions invite dialogue without accusation. In many congregations, there are people or groups of people who have great ties to particular ministries or memories. While your plan may address the question of how these ministries or memories affect your current reality, it is important to address your questions in ways that do not undermine the integrity of people or groups of people in your church. This does not mean that your Promised Land Task Force should avoid asking necessary and important questions. It does mean that your task force should ask these questions in ways that invite all people in your church to dialogue toward consensus. For many churches where conversations and communications happen in parking lots, behind closed Sunday school doors, through telephone calls, and through emails, this will require a new understanding of accountability for discussions and decisions made by the church body. If a congregation is going to enter God's Promised Land of discipleship, its members must intentionally choose to ask the right questions that will allow them to model the redeemed need to serve rather than the human need to win. They must empty themselves of their own agendas as they take on the nature and mission of Jesus Christ. To enter God's Promised Land for Jesus' disciples, a church must align its current reality to Jesus' envisioned reality. Asking the right questions, your strategic-ministry plan will need to extend this invitation to your church.

If your Promised Land Task Force determines that the current reality of your church does not align with Jesus' envisioned reality, then your strategic-ministry plan will need to recommend goals of how you can live into a new reality. The intent of these goals will be the transformation of your church so that it may live in the vision and mission for which Jesus prayed. You will introduce this invitation to transformation through the development of a mission statement, through assessment of your church's current reality, and by asking right questions. Your church will accept this invitation to transformation through the approval of goals defined by related activities and desired outcomes that your strategic-ministry plan presents.

A strategic-ministry plan incorporates activities that lead to desired outcomes that are measurable. Often, churches focus inwardly on the implementation of an activity (i.e., a church program) rather than on a specific, measurable outcome that nurtures and equips people to be followers of Jesus. A church focused on activities plans a vacation Bible school for the needs of its own children. A church focused on desired outcomes plans a vacation Bible school that looks beyond its own needs to the needs of children in the community.

Plan your activities and desired outcomes within a two-year timeframe. This timeframe will make your goals attainable and accountable:

    a. Develop action plans with desired outcomes that will help your church to align itself to Jesus' prayer in John 17 by:

      i.   Arranging desired behaviors, tasks, programs and outcomes on timeline;

      ii. Assigning specific responsibilities;

      iii. Assigning deliverable milestones.

    (Download an "Action Plan Template" at www.upperroom.org/bookstore/ prayer/ActionPlan.pdf or at www.faithfulljourney.org).

    b. Recommending to the church's governing body a team responsible for the oversight progress toward approved goals.

In recommending specific outcomes, it is critical to measure them through the vision and mission of Jesus' prayer for his disciples. Align goals to the vision of living in joy and unity for the glory of God and to the mission of living as followers of Jesus sent into the world if they will help your church to live into a new reality. State goals clearly and concisely. They should offer the hope of how your church can become a transforming symbol of God's presence to people who are searching for hope in their lives. Your recommended goals should offer a vision of how your church can overcome the giants that are facing it as it seeks to enter God's Promised Land for Jesus' disciples. Some goals may be general in nature and some goals may be specific in nature, but the goals you recommend must offer an invitation to a new vision for your church's existence.

Desired outcomes will provide a roadmap of accountability for the ministry plan that your church adopts. Framed within timelines and desired results, desired outcomes assign specific expectations and responsibilities that allow goals to become realities. The "Action Plan Template" in (see www.upperroom.org/bookstore/prayer/ActionPlan.pdf or www.faithfulljourney.org) is designed to assist your Promised Land Task Force in determining activities, desired outcomes, timeframes, and responsible parties.

To ensure that your church's strategic-ministry plan becomes the guiding focus of your church, your report should include recommendations for approval and oversight by the appropriate governing body. Create a ministry team for the sole responsibility of overseeing the implementation of the approved plan. Each time this governing body meets, the team should provide an update and reports on the execution of the plan. (The "Action Plan Template" available online can assist in the documentation of progress.) In turn, provide the congregation with regular updates to keep the vision of Jesus' envisioned reality clear. Chapter eleven in unit three includes a process for oversight and implementation of the strategic-ministry plan.

Step 6: Achieve Congregational Consensus

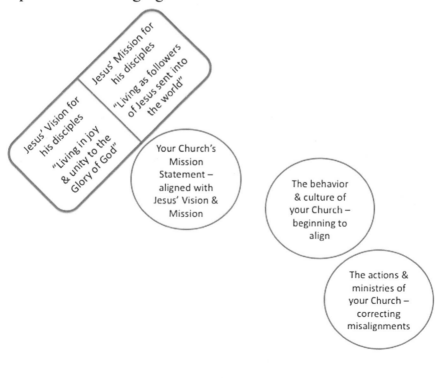

The desired outcome of your strategic-ministry plan is a congregation that aligns itself with the vision and mission of Jesus' prayer. This transformational alignment will occur only as the congregation achieves consensus. Such transformation takes time, patience, flexibility, grace, steadfastness, and perseverance as people faithfully remember, are faithfully equipped, and are faithfully encouraged to live into the reality that the strategic-ministry plan advances.

Consensus will occur as people allow their relationships with each other to influence their goal of entering God's Promised Land for Jesus' disciples. Following Paul's advice to the Philippians, people in your faith community must be of the same mind as they align their lives to the tasks to which God has called them. Doing nothing out of selfish ambition or conceit, they must look not only to their own interests but instead to the interests of others as they have the mind of Christ among them as a community of faith. People in your church will need to agree that the vision of your church is to live in joy and unity in Jesus to the glory of God with the mission of being followers of Jesus sent into the world.

Your Promised Land Task Force has been entrusted with helping to lead your congregation in achieving consensus about this vision and mission. As transformational leaders, you will help to influence and shape the present and future opinion of your congregation regarding the strategic-ministry plan. In fulfilling the responsibility of transformational leadership, you will need to model the qualities of leadership that you will be asking your congregation to model: remembering encouragement, ability to ask the right questions, ability to see beyond self-focused concerns, and leading by the redeemed need to serve.

A two-step feedback process will achieve consensus. Your task force will first present the strategic-ministry plan to your church's governing body for reflection with appropriate revisions being made to the plan. The revised plan will then be presented at a congregation-wide meeting for interaction and feedback. This is a critical step in achieving congregational consensus as their feedback is incorporated into the completed strategic-ministry plan. The following chapter focuses on this congregational presentation by the Promised Land Task Force. As you fulfill this faith-sized responsibility, remember that Jesus has already prayed for your church and for you.

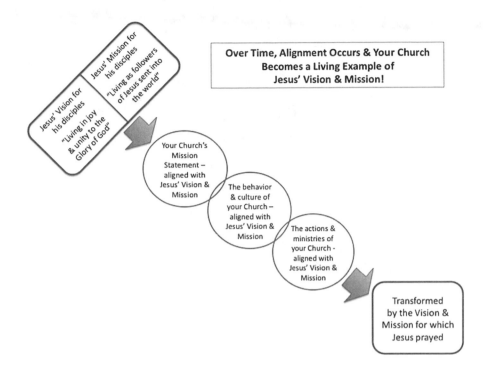

Jesus' Vision for his disciples "Living in joy & unity to the Glory of God"

Jesus' Mission for his disciples "Living as followers of Jesus sent into the world"

Over Time, Alignment Occurs & Your Church Becomes a Living Example of Jesus' Vision & Mission!

Your Church's Mission Statement – aligned with Jesus' Vision & Mission

The behavior & culture of your Church – aligned with Jesus' Vision & Mission

The actions & ministries of your Church - aligned with Jesus' Vision & Mission

Transformed by the Vision & Mission for which Jesus prayed

UNIT THREE

CHAPTER TEN

Presenting to the Congregation

Acts 2 tells the story of the birth of the church. Disciples who had followed Jesus in his earthly ministry became apostles as they proclaimed the radical truth of the risen Christ. People who had run away from Jesus' invitation to take up their cross and follow him were now lifting up the cross of Jesus for the world to see. Empowered by the Holy Spirit, they began to speak one common message about God's deeds of power in Jesus. In a miraculous moment as the apostles spoke in languages they did not understand, but that was not the biggest miracle of Pentecost. The biggest miracle of Pentecost was that people from different backgrounds and life experiences began to ask the same question, "What does this mean," as the Spirit drew them to the story of God's love spoken through Jesus:

> When the day of Pentecost had come, they were all together in one place. And suddenly from heaven there came a sound like the rush of a violent wind, and it filled the entire house where they were sitting. Divided tongues, as of fire, appeared among them, and a tongue rested on each of them. All of them were filled with the Holy Spirit and began to speak in other languages, as the Spirit gave them ability.

Now there were devout Jews from every nation under heaven living in Jerusalem. And at this sound the crowd gathered and was bewildered, because each one heard them speaking in the native language of each. Amazed and astonished, they asked, "Are not all these who are speaking Galileans? And how is it that we hear, each of us, in our own native language? Parthians, Medes, Elamites, and residents of Mesopotamia, Judea and Cappadocia, Pontus and Asia, Phrygia and Pamphylia, Egypt and the parts of Libya belonging to Cyrene, and visitors from Rome, both Jews and proselytes, Cretans and Arabs—in our own languages we hear them speaking about God's deeds of power." All were amazed and perplexed, saying to one another, "What does this mean?" (Acts 2:1-12).

As your Promised Land Task Force presents the strategic-ministry plan discerned for your congregation, your goal is for the miracle of Pentecost to happen in the life of your church. Pentecost will happen as your task force speaks the same message about God's deeds of power through the different languages of your church. Your church will realize the power of the Holy Spirit as the Spirit draws people from different backgrounds and life experiences to the story of God's love spoken through Jesus. For this to happen, your task force will need to speak one common message as you present a strategic-ministry plan that helps your church draw people to Jesus. Through your presentation, you will want people from the various tribes of your congregation to ask the same question about what this plan means for the vision and mission of your church.

In presenting your Promised Land Task Force's report, you will need to consider prayerfully how the presentation of your strategic-ministry plan can help people in your church to ask the right question that is the focus of Jesus' prayer for his disciples, **"How can we glorify God through our life together?"** To help your people ask this right question, your task force will need to discern the questions that you need to address through your presentation, questions like:

- Does our presentation clearly share the vision and mission of Jesus' prayer for his disciples?

- Do the vision and mission statements we are proposing align with the vision and mission of Jesus' prayer for his disciples?

- How can we invite dialogue rather than debate about the current reality of our church?

- What questions do we need to ask that will help people objectively and fairly receive our presentation about the giants our church is facing?

- How can we help people ask right questions so that our church can live into the envisioned reality of God's Promised Land for Jesus' disciples?

Determine who will present the ministry plan to your congregation. Your primary presenters should be respected leaders of your church. They should be able to articulate clearly an understanding of the strategic-ministry plan that will generate trust in the work of the task force. In addition to determining the primary presenters, select the people who will be the primary responders to questions that people in the congregation may be asked. If you are using assessment documents provided by FaithFull Journey, LLC regarding the current reality of your church, determine how you will incorporate this material into your presentation. Your task force will need to ensure that the congregation understands the governing system that your church practices. All announcements related to the presentation should clearly state the method by which the church will approve the plan.

Suggested Agenda for Presenting Your Plan

1) Open with a prayer seeking God's blessing and guidance.

2) Introduce Promised Land Task Force members.

3) Review biblical foundations that formed the plan. Briefly outline each of the passages using the synopsis of Bible studies found in Appendix 3.

   a. Jesus' prayer for his disciples: John 17.

   b. Choosing between envisioned reality and perceived reality: Numbers 13:1-14:9.

   c. Overcoming giants: Numbers 13:25-14:9.

   d. Asking the right questions: Mark 9:30-35.

   e. Beyond and within: Mark 8:34-37.

   f. Entering God's Promised Land: Philippians 2:1-11.

4) Review how the plan was determined using the biblical model in Acts 6:1-7 found in Bible study five.

   a. Define the mission of the congregation.

   b.   Assess current reality through mission values.

   c.   Organize a response through consultation with leadership.

   d.   Achieve consensus by the congregation that will enable current reality to be transformed by unity of vision and consensus of mission.

5) Present the plan along with recommendations.

   a.   Share Jesus' envisioned reality for his disciples.

       i.   Vision—living in joy and unity in Jesus to the glory of God: specific vision statement being recommended for your church.

       ii. Mission—followers of Jesus sent into the world specific mission statement being recommended for your church.

   b.   Assess your church's current reality.

   c.   Identify the giants facing your church.

   d.   State the questions that need to be answered in order for your church to overcome the giants that are facing it.

   e.   Share how this plan will help your church to align its vision for ministry through the biblical principle of *Beyond and Within*.

   f.   Share how this plan will help your church to glorify God as it enters God's Promised Land for Jesus' disciples.

6) Questions and answers.

7) Summary statement.

8) Explain next steps being recommended for the implementation of the plan.

   a.   Possible revisions based on congregational feedback.

   b.   Presentation of the revised plan for approval by the appropriate governing structure of your local church.

9) Close with prayer.

In presenting the ministry plan, it is essential that your Promised Land Task Force be open and non-defensive in your response to questions and concerns. It is your task force's responsibility to explain the process by which you discerned the ministry plan. Your task force, however, does not have the responsibility for defending the process by which the ministry plan was discerned. By following the steps outlined in this book, the process that has been followed was approved by the appropriate governing body of your church. If people question your assessment of the current reality or the giants of your church, explain that your assessment was based on responses received by small-group Bible-study participants and by statistical information that reflects the recent history of your church. If people question the recommendations of the Promised Land Task Force, state that the recommendations discerned by the task force are being presented to the whole congregation for its discernment and ultimate approval through the appropriate governing structure of your church. Feedback from your congregation is important as it may provide perspectives that will help refine your strategic plan. The outcome that your task force desires is a plan that *invites dialogue* and ultimately helps people in your church to ask the right question: "How can we glorify God through our life together?"

It is important that your Promised Land Task Force model the envisioned reality for which Jesus prayed for the community of disciples who form your church. As you prepare for this responsibility, review together the envisioned reality that Paul described for the church in Philippians 2:1-4:

> If then there is any encouragement in Christ, any consolation from love, any sharing in the Spirit, any compassion and sympathy, make my joy complete: be of the same mind, having the same love, being in full accord and of one mind. Do nothing from selfish ambition or conceit, but in humility regard others as better than yourselves. Let each of you look not to your own interests, but to the interests of others.

Let these words of encouragement be the prayer and vision of your Promised Land Task Force as you perfect your church's strategic-ministry plan through congregational consensus and subsequent approval by your church's governing body.

UNIT THREE

CHAPTER ELEVEN

Living in God's Promised Land

Faith is an eternal conversation with God, who has spoken from the beginning. The initial verses of Genesis record the beginning words of this conversation as God said, "Let there be light." To understand the full impact of these words, it is crucial to realize that while God created light on the first day in Genesis 1:3, God did not speak the sun and moon into existence until the fourth day of creation in Genesis 1:16. The creation of light before the creation of the sun and moon is an invitation for humanity to understand that life depends upon God. While the rising and setting of the sun may order our days, God orders our lives, in the same way God brought order out of chaos:

> In the beginning when God created the heavens and the earth, the earth was a formless void and darkness covered the face of the deep, while a wind from God swept over the face of the waters. Then God said, "Let there be light"; and there was light. And God saw that the light was good; and God separated the light from the darkness. God called the light Day, and the darkness he called Night. And there was evening and there was morning, the first day (Genesis 1:1-5).

Followers of Jesus understand the meaning of having God order their lives. The prologue to John's Gospel in John 1:1-18 speaks to our faith in the holy conversation that became flesh in Jesus, the light of the world. Some of the verses in John's prologue that speak to this faith are:

> In the beginning was the Word, and the Word was with God, and the Word was God. He was in the beginning with God. All things came into being through him, and without him not one thing came into being. What has come into being in him was life, and the life was the light of all people. The light shines in the darkness, and the darkness did not overcome it (John 1:1-5).

> And the Word became flesh and lived among us, and we have seen his glory, the glory as of a father's only son, full of grace and truth . . . (John 1:14).

Jesus' disciples seek to order their lives through their faith in Jesus. Connecting the stories of their lives with the story of God's eternal conversation with creation, they believe in the Word that became flesh in their Savior. This statement of faith nurtures and equips them on their journey to God's Promised Land of discipleship.

As your church lives into its strategic-ministry plan, it is crucial for your community of faith to understand that the approved plan is a statement of faith that will guide your congregation on its journey to God's Promised Land of discipleship. While your approved plan contains goals and desired outcomes intended to order the strategic ministry of your church, the church needs to interpret it as a prayerful process of spiritual discernment founded on scripture. Remember that the desired outcome of your task force's work is a strategic-ministry plan that invites dialogue and ultimately helps people in your church to ask the right question, **"How can we glorify God through our life together."** This right question invites people to connect the individual stories of their lives with the larger biblical story of life.

After the church approves the strategic-ministry plan, your task force's assigned responsibility will be completed. While your assigned responsibility may be completed, your ministry is not. It is important that you continue to encourage your church to be faithful in implementing the strategic-ministry plan. As the church continues to implement the goals and desired outcomes of the strategic-ministry plan, members of your task force will need to continue modeling the four traits of leadership that guided your work: remembering encouragement, ability to ask the right questions, ability to see beyond self-focused concerns, and leading by the redeemed need to serve. These leadership traits formed the criteria for your task force's self-assessment as they wrote your strategic-ministry plan. The plan invites your congregation to display these same traits as it lives into the reality that the approved plan envisions.

Most strategic-ministry plans look great on paper. Living into the reality they envision is a different matter. This is why many strategic plans end up on shelves as relics of possibilities. While they may envision desired outcomes, they do not address the foundational choices that the church must make in order to experience a new reality. They do not teach a new language that will empower different voices of concern to ask the same question. The strategic-ministry plan addresses foundational realities and invites your church to ask the right question about the reality Jesus has envisioned for your community of disciples. Some people in your church will begin to speak a new language as their individual concerns align with a larger vision. Some people in your church will respond in ways that seek to protect their individual concerns. As your church implements the ministry plan, members of your task force and the team that oversees the plan's implementation will need to keep asking the right question, **"How can we glorify God through our life together?"**

Living into the reality Jesus envisioned in his prayer for his disciples, your task force's continuing ministry is remembering encouragement as you ask right questions, see beyond self-focused concerns, and lead by the redeemed need to serve. When tempted to engage in power struggles, remember that your intent resides in your questions. Guided by the biblical principle of *Beyond and Within*, look beyond your church's current reality through a vision of discipleship that transforms present values. Following Jesus' admonition for his disciples to lose their lives for his sake and the gospel's, lead by sharing the love of God that focuses beyond your own concerns. This focus enables transformation. Engage in faithful conversation that expresses the grace and truth of God's Word becoming flesh in Jesus as you follow Jesus' sacrificial example of love. Remind your church of the vision of God's Promised Land that Philippians 2:1-4 describes:

> If then there is any encouragement in Christ, any consolation from love, any sharing in the Spirit, any compassion and sympathy, make my joy complete: be of the same mind, having the same love, being in full accord and of one mind. Do nothing from selfish ambition or conceit, but in humility regard others as better than yourselves. Let each of you look not to your own interests, but to the interests of others.

This Promised Land of discipleship forms your church's covenant response to the strategic-ministry plan. In turn, a vision of living in joy and unity in Jesus will empower your church. Answering the right question of how your church can glorify God through your life together, a common mission of living as followers of Jesus sent into the world can define your church. To live faithfully in this Promised Land, your church's ministry will need to be part of God's eternal conversation spoken from the beginning. As your church engages in this conversation, people beyond your congregation will begin to ask about the transformation that they are witnessing as your church lives a missionary faith. In turn, these people will realize that God is inviting them to join in an eternal conversation that is transformational as faith in Jesus orders their lives.

Just as the opening chapter of the biblical story of faith speaks of God's eternal conversation with creation, the closing chapter of the Bible speaks of God's eternal conversation of faith. Revelation 22:1-5 speaks to this eternal conversation by bearing witness to the creative power of God who said, "Let there be light" and the redeeming power of God spoken through Jesus:

> Then the angel showed me the river of the water of life, bright as crystal, flowing from the throne of God and of the Lamb through the middle of the street of the city. On either side of the river is the tree of life with its twelve kinds of fruit, producing its fruit each month; and the leaves of the tree are for the healing of the nations. Nothing accursed will be found there any more. But the throne of God and of the Lamb will be in it, and his servants will worship him; they will see his face, and his name will be on their foreheads. And there will be no more night; they need no light of lamp or sun, for the Lord God will be their light, and they will reign forever and ever.

When a congregation understands that the light of God in Jesus defines its vision, a new day of ministry begins. Living into the promise of an envisioned reality, a community of faith joins an eternal conversation that begins and ends with God as it answers the question, **"How can we glorify God through our life together?"**

As your church considers how it shall enter God's Promised Land of discipleship by responding to this question, remember that Jesus has already prayed for your answer.

Process Overview Graphic

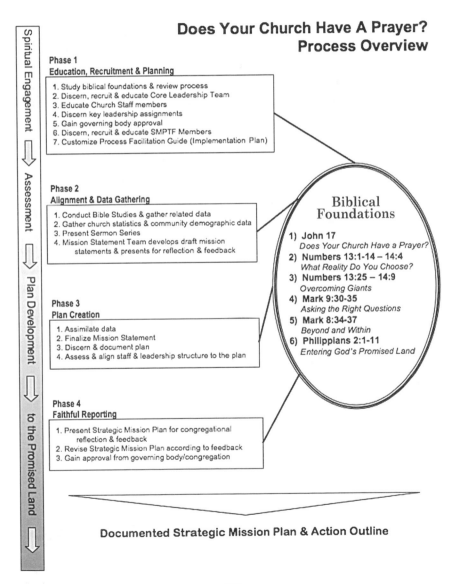

Does Your Church Have A Prayer?
Process Overview

Spiritual Engagement ⇩ Assessment ⇩ Plan Development ⇩ to the Promised Land ⇩

Phase 1
Education, Recruitment & Planning

1. Study biblical foundations & review process
2. Discern, recruit & educate Core Leadership Team
3. Educate Church Staff members
4. Discern key leadership assignments
5. Gain governing body approval
6. Discern, recruit & educate SMPTF Members
7. Customize Process Facilitation Guide (Implementation Plan)

Phase 2
Alignment & Data Gathering

1. Conduct Bible Studies & gather related data
2. Gather church statistics & community demographic data
3. Present Sermon Series
4. Mission Statement Team develops draft mission
   statements & presents for reflection & feedback

Phase 3
Plan Creation

1. Assimilate data
2. Finalize Mission Statement
3. Discern & document plan
4. Assess & align staff & leadership structure to the plan

Phase 4
Faithful Reporting

1. Present Strategic Mission Plan for congregational
   reflection & feedback
2. Revise Strategic Mission Plan according to feedback
3. Gain approval from governing body/congregation

Biblical Foundations

1) **John 17**
   Does Your Church Have a Prayer?
2) **Numbers 13:1-14 – 14:4**
   What Reality Do You Choose?
3) **Numbers 13:25 – 14:9**
   Overcoming Giants
4) **Mark 9:30-35**
   Asking the Right Questions
5) **Mark 8:34-37**
   Beyond and Within
6) **Philippians 2:1-11**
   Entering God's Promised Land

Documented Strategic Mission Plan & Action Outline

APPENDIX 2

Sermon Outlines

Preaching is an act of faith. Painting on the canvas of scripture, preachers tell the story of sin and redemption, tragedy and hope, death and resurrection. Within the rich colors and hues of the Christian faith, preachers connect Jesus' present generation of disciples with the ongoing story of God's love. Interwoven in this fabric of divine hope preachers have the sacred responsibility of sharing the message of salvation. As Paul describes this task:

> For since, in the wisdom of God, the world did not know God through wisdom, it pleased God through the folly of what we preach to save those who believe (1 Corinthians 1:21).

The following sermon outlines can assist you in telling the story of God's ongoing conversation with creation. Each week you will communicate the message of a Savior who prayed for his followers as he looked over into God's Promised Land of discipleship. As the spiritual leader, you will guide your congregation on a holy journey that will help people in your church hear with ears of faith as they follow Jesus. As you craft your sermons, remember that Jesus has prayed for your church and for you.

Week One Sermon: Jesus Prayed for You
John 17:1-5, 13-26

Introduction

The focus of this sermon is to help Jesus' followers understand that Jesus has prayed for them. John 17 provides the setting for the sermon as Jesus prays for his disciples who have followed him in his earthly ministry and for his disciples who will follow him in his resurrected ministry. The context of Jesus' prayer is the Garden of Gethsemane as Jesus is preparing himself for the glory of his crucifixion. As he prays, Jesus envisions a Promised Land of discipleship where his followers will be guided by the vision of God's love that is guiding him to the mission of the cross.

Jesus prays his disciples will understand the vision and mission of the glory of his crucifixion. By understanding that Jesus has prayed for them, Jesus' disciples can live in the vision and mission of Jesus' calling upon their lives. Jesus' high priestly prayer in John 17 is Jesus' vision and mission statement for his disciples.

Points to Consider

Point One: Jesus prayed for your church and for the people who form the fellowship of your church when he prayed for the disciples who followed him in his earthly ministry and for the disciples who follow him in his resurrected ministry:

> I ask not only on behalf of these, but also on behalf of those who
> will believe in me through their word (v.20).

Jesus' prayer forms Jesus' vision statement for his disciples and for your congregation. There are three foundations of Jesus' prayer that form Jesus' vision for his disciples.

The first foundation is the vision of Jesus' disciples growing and being formed in the truth of God's love that is revealed through Jesus:

> Sanctify them in the truth; your word is truth (v.17).

> And for their sakes I sanctify myself, so that they also may be sanctified in truth (v19).

The second foundation is a vision of joy as Jesus' disciples focus their lives on the love that guided Jesus to the cross:

> But now I am coming to you, and I speak these things in the world
> so that they may have my joy made complete in themselves (v.13).

The third foundation is a vision of unity as Jesus' disciples are united in God's love that is revealed through Jesus:

> I ask not only on behalf of these, but also on behalf of those who
> will believe in me through their word, that they may all be one. As
> you, Father, are in me and I am in you, may they also be in us, so
> that the world may believe that you have sent me (vs.20-21).

> Father, I desire that those also, whom you have given me, may be
> with me where I am, to see my glory, which you have given me
> because you loved me before the foundation of the world (v.24).

Point Two: Jesus' prayer forms Jesus' mission statement for his disciples
and for your congregation. There are three foundations of Jesus' prayer that
form Jesus' mission for his disciples:

The first foundation is Jesus' disciples living as followers of Jesus sent into
the world:

> As you have sent me into the world, so I have sent them into the
> world (v.18).

The second foundation is Jesus' disciples living as witnesses of God's love
so that the world may believe that God sent Jesus through the lives of Jesus'
disciples:

> The glory that you have given me I have given them, so that they
> may be one, as we are one, I in them and you in me, that they may
> become completely one, so that the world may know that you have
> sent me and have loved them even as you have loved me (vs.22-23).

The third foundation is Jesus' disciples living as people who are sent in the
same sending love that led Jesus to the cross:

> Righteous Father, the world does not know you, but I know you;
> and these know that you have sent me. I made your name known to
> them, and I will make it known, so that the love with which you
> have loved me may be in them, and I in them (vs.25-26).

Possible Sermon Starters

Tell of a time when you understood that prayer made a difference in your life.

SERMON STARTER ONE

Life is challenging. Can anyone disagree? It's true. Our lives are wrought with
an array of difficult and challenging situations. At varying times in our lives, we
have all tried to deal with these on our own. We tell ourselves, "I don't want
to bother someone else with my troubles" or "No one really cares about my
troubles." As our faith starts to shape our lives, however, we begin to see life
through a different lens, from a larger perspective than our own. Living in
relationship with God and within a faith community changes everything. Can
you recall the first time you knew that someone outside your family truly

cared for you in your time of trouble? Can you remember the first time some-one cared enough to tell you they would pray for you in your time of need?

I recall the first time I internalized these expressions of care as an adult. It was an important point in my faith journey. How does it make you feel to know someone in our faith community is praying for you? Did you know that Jesus prayed for you in the Garden of Gethsemane? It's true, Jesus prayed for you and me over 2000 years ago while he was still on this earth.

Sermon Starter Two

Have you noticed in our monthly newsletter (weekly bulletin, or during our worship services) how many people are moved to thank our community of faith for our prayers and support during an especially trying time? As people of faith, we deeply appreciate the prayers of others because we know the power prayer has in our lives. During a hospital visit one day, an older parish-ioner gave me a beautiful image of what prayer meant to her. She said, "It feels as though I am being lifted up to God on the hands of those who care for me." What a beautiful image. Think with me for a moment: how does it make you feel to know someone is praying for you? How would it make you feel to know that Jesus prayed for you while still on this earth, while in the Garden of Gethsemane? In John 17, we have the account of Jesus praying for you and me over 2000 years ago.

Week Two Sermon: What Reality Do You Choose?
Numbers 13:17–14:9

Introduction

The premise of this sermon is that the story of Israel's response to the report of the twelve spies is an analogy of today's church. The congregation of Israel had to choose the interpretation of reality in which they would reside as they received two differing interpretations of the Promised Land from the spies. Hearing the ten spies who reported through their self-perceptions and the two spies who reported through their vision of God's promise, the congregation of Israel chose the report of the ten spies. Today's congregations also must choose the interpretation of reality in which they will live out their ministry. The real-ity they choose will either cause them to wander in search of a reason for their existence or lead them to the Promised Land for which Jesus prayed for his disciples in John 17.

Points to Consider

Point One: Israel was standing on the edge of a new reality. The Promised Land was before them: a land that flowed with milk and honey, a land with untold potential. The twelve spies were in consensus about the potential of the reality they observed:

> And they came to the Wadi Eshcol, and cut down from there a branch with a single cluster of grapes, and they carried it on a pole between two of them. They also brought some pomegranates and figs. That place was called the Wadi Eshcol, because of the cluster that the Israelites cut down from there. At the end of forty days they returned from spying out the land. And they came to Moses and Aaron and to all the congregation of the Israelites in the wilderness of Paran, at Kadesh; they brought back word to them and to all the congregation, and showed them the fruit of the land. And they told him, "We came to the land to which you sent us; it flows with milk and honey, and this is its fruit" (13:23-27).

Charged with the responsibility of providing an objective assessment of the present reality that was before Israel, these spies also had the responsibility of interpreting that reality. While all of the spies agreed on the reality they saw, ten of the spies thought the challenges of the Promised Land were too great for Israel. Two of the spies thought that God's past faithfulness was sufficient for overcoming the challenges of the Promised Land.

> "Yet the people who live in the land are strong, and the towns are fortified and very large; and besides, we saw the descendants of Anak there. The Amalekites live in the land of the Negeb; the Hittites, the Jebusites, and the Amorites live in the hill country; and the Canaanites live by the sea, and along the Jordan." But Caleb quieted the people before Moses, and said, "Let us go up at once and occupy it, for we are well able to overcome it" (13:28-30).

Like the congregation of Israel, today's congregations face a reality they have never encountered before. Today's congregations need an objective assessment of their present reality. After assessing their present reality, they also have the responsibility of interpreting reality based on the promise and vision of God's presence. Perceived reality and envisioned reality define the differing interpretations of reality between the ten spies and the two spies.

The ten spies interpreted reality through their self-limiting perceptions. Reporting on the reality of giants in the Promised Land, the ten spies felt inadequate to meet the challenges before them. Focusing on the inadequacy of their self-perceptions rather than on God's promised future for Abraham, they could not see beyond the present reality of the giants nor could their vision see beyond themselves. As a result, the spies' present perception of seeming like grasshoppers to the giants and to themselves controlled their response to the future that had been promised by God:

> Then the men who had gone up with him said, "We are not able to go up against this people, for they are stronger than we." So they brought to the Israelites an unfavorable report of the land that they had spied out, saying, "The land that we have gone through as spies is a land that devours its inhabitants; and all the people that we saw in it are of great size. There we saw the Nephilim (the Anakites come from the Nephilim); and to ourselves we seemed like grasshoppers, and so we seemed to them" (13:31-33).

Caleb and Joshua interpreted reality through their present trust in God's future faithfulness; Joshua and Caleb encouraged the congregation of Israel to face the giants of the Promised Land without fear. Where the ten spies saw the reality of the Promised Land through their perceived fears of the giants, Joshua and Caleb saw the reality of the Promised Land through their envisioned trust in God. Because of their envisioned reality, the focus of these two spies was on God rather than of the giants of the Promised Land:

> But Caleb quieted the people before Moses, and said, "Let us go up at once and occupy it, for we are well able to overcome it" (13:30).

> The land that we went through as spies is an exceedingly good land. If the LORD is pleased with us, he will bring us into this land and give it to us, a land that flows with milk and honey. Only, do not rebel against the LORD; and do not fear the people of the land, for they are no more than bread for us; their protection is removed from them, and the LORD is with us; do not fear them" (14:7-9).

Point Two: Israel chose to live in perceived reality. As a result, Israel wandered in a wilderness of death for forty years. As a congregation plans its ministries, it must choose between perceived reality and envisioned reality. Like the congregation of Israel, its choice of reality will determine whether it wanders in search of a reason for its existence or enters God's Promised Land for disciples of Jesus Christ.

Possible Sermon Starters

SERMON STARTER ONE

We live in such an affluent society that having choices has moved from being a joy to being a challenge and nuisance. Gone are the days when your mate glibly asks you to pick up some shampoo. You cannot simply go to the store and find shampoo, because you must choose from shampoo with the essence of fruit, or fortified with this or that, or for every conceivable hair type or condition. You cannot simply ask for or find shampoo. Similarly we cannot simply ask for a cup of coffee. No, now we must decide . . . decaf or regular, skim, 2%, whole milk, or how about cream? Is that cream flavored? Which flavor from our array of choices do you prefer? How about a cola? Oh yes. Do you want it sugar-free, calorie-free, or caffeine-free; would you like your cola lime, vanilla, or cherry-flavored?

We start making choices as little children. What flavor of ice cream do I want? What color of fingerpaints will I use? Will I add a mural to the wall with my fingerpaints? Because of our many choices, we must make a myriad of decisions each and every day. Many are insignificant, yet others may affect us for a lifetime.

Decision-making is especially difficult when there is no consensus, and risk looms high. At these times we must make hard choices. Do we concede to satisfy the vocal onslaught of the majority, or do we have faith and conviction to go against the majority view?

Moses and the people of Israel stood on the edge of the Promised Land, and they had a hard choice to make. Where will they put their faith? Do they follow the consensus of the ten spies, or do they follow the two and put their faith and trust in their experience with God? Will they choose based on their fears, or will they choose as they look through the lens of God's promise?

As faith communities, the people of God today, we too have hard choices to make.

SERMON STARTER TWO

We live in a time when having choices has moved from being a joy to being a challenge and nuisance. Gone are the days when your mate glibly asks you to pick us up some shampoo. You cannot simply go to the store and find shampoo, because you must choose from shampoo with the essence of fruit, or fortified with this or that, or for every conceivable hair type or condition, but you cannot simply ask for or find shampoo. Also, we cannot simply ask for a cup of coffee. No, now we must decide . . . decaf or regular, skim, 2%, whole milk, or how about cream? Is that cream flavored? Which flavor from our array of choices do you prefer? Or how about a cola? Oh yes. Do you want it sugar-free, calorie-free, or caffeine-free; would you like your cola lime, vanilla, or cherry-flavored?

We start making choices as little children. What flavor of ice cream do I want? What color of finger paints will I use? Will I add a mural to the wall with my finger paints? As adults, choices become a significant part of our daily lives. Because of our many choices, we must make a myriad of decisions each and every day. Many are insignificant, yet others may affect us for a lifetime.

John Briggs, one of the authors of "Does You Church Have a Prayer," counts his entry into pastoral ministry at age forty-nine as one of those life-changing decisions. He had the choice of continuing in business or choosing to follow the path of God's call. He speaks of having to deal with the fear of the unknown and the accompanying anxiety as he struggled to make the right choice. How can one begin to make such monumental decisions?

In making significant decisions, most of us begin by reasoning through the choices with the advice and counsel of trusted advisers. But in the end, even with the best of counsel, we cannot know the future, and we make our choice in hope and faith. We either put our hope and faith in our ability to make the right choice, or we put our faith and hope in the promises of God to lead.

This is where Moses and the people of Israel stood as they considered entering God's Promised Land. They, too, had a hard choice to make. Where will they put their hope and faith? Do they follow the consensus of the ten spies, or do they follow the two and put their hope and faith in their experiences with God? Will they choose based on their fears, or will they choose to look through the lens of God's promise?

Week Three Sermon: Overcoming Giants
Numbers 13:25–14:9

Introduction

This sermon invites a congregation to consider how it will assess and overcome the giants that are dwelling in the Promised Land that Jesus envisioned through his prayer in John 17. While the sermon will identify some general giants that are facing the church, it will invite people to think about some of the giants that are facing their particular church. The goal of the sermon is to help a congregation focus beyond the giants to the vision and mission of living as God's sent people.

Points to Consider

Point One: All of the spies agreed on the reality they saw in the Promised Land: a land flowing with milk and honey. They also agreed on the challenge of the reality they saw: there were giants who dwelled in the Promised Land. Some of the giants who were dwelling in the Promised Land were general in nature:

> Then the men who had gone up with him said, "We are not able to go up against this people, for they are stronger than we." So they brought to the Israelites an unfavorable report of the land that they had spied out, saying, "The land that we have gone through as spies is a land that devours its inhabitants; and all the people that we saw in it are of great size" (13:31-32).

Some of the giants dwelling in the Promised Land were specific in nature. The spies' report included people who were known to the congregation of Israel as Nephilim. The mere mention of their presence by the spies was enough to cause the congregation of Israel to focus on their self-perceived limitations rather than to live into the vision of God's promise for them.

> "There we saw the Nephilim (the Anakites come from the Nephilim); and to ourselves we seemed like grasshoppers, and so we seemed to them" (13:33).

Point Two: If a church is going to live in the Promised Land that Jesus envisioned for his faithful disciples, it will also need to overcome giants. Some of these giants are general in nature and face every congregation. Bible study three reviews three of these general giants. The first general giant is worldviews as referenced by Walter Wink in *The Powers That Be, Theology for a New Millennium*. These worldviews are ancient, spiritualist, materialist, theological, and integral. Wink summarizes his thoughts on these worldviews by stating, "The important point here is that we may be the first generation in the history of the world that can make a conscious choice between these worldviews" (Walter Wink, *The Powers That Be, Theology for a New Millennium*, [New York: Galilee Doubleday, 1999], 22). The second general giant is technology and the expectations it raises. While technology raises expectations for making life more manageable, it cannot speak to the basic meaning of life that is beyond human knowledge. The third giant is expectation. People have expectations by which they measure relevancy as they value meaning and worth for their lives. It is at the crossroads of expectations that the church has the holy responsibility of helping people understand their meaning and worth through the eternal story of God's love in

Jesus Christ. A congregation must help people envision a life that is beyond their expectations as it connects them with the eternal message of God's love in ways that are relevant to the present challenges of life.

Point Three: Some of the giants that dwell in the Promised Land Jesus envisioned for his disciples are specific to the context of particular churches. The mere mention of their presence can cause these congregations to focus on their self-perceived limitations rather than to live into the vision of God's promise for them. When allowed, specific giants can cause members to focus within their own concerns of institutional survival rather than looking beyond themselves as missional expressions of God's Holy Spirit. Instead of living as people who are envisioned by God's promise of faithfulness for Jesus disciples, their self-perceptions control them.

Point Four: To overcome the general and specific giants that a congregation faces, it must focus on living as people sent into the world through the power of God's love and the promise of God's faithfulness. Intentional choices must be made that will allow a congregation to structure itself to see beyond the giants and comprehend future possibilities for ministry that will be empowered by God. Congregations that are able to overcome the giants that face them live as communities of Jesus' disciples who glorify God by their very existence.

Possible Sermon Starters

SERMON STARTER ONE

The English fairy tale of *Jack and the Beanstalk* has been a favorite of children since it was written in the early 1800s. You remember the story. Jack trades his cow for a handful of magical beans. His mother can't believe it and becomes furious, throwing the beans out of the door. Jack is sent to bed with no supper, but the next morning he awakens to find a giant beanstalk growing all the way to the sky. He climbs and climbs in search of a great fortune. He finds only a giant ogre stands in his way of getting a goose that lays a golden egg and a golden harp. It's a story of how Jack deals with the giant ogre in order to get his fortune.

I am struck with how this story parallels the lives of our young people when they complete their schooling and begin their careers. In a sense they, too, seek their fortunes. As they climb up the ladder of their selected fields, what are the giants that they will encounter? How will they deal with the giants they will surely face? Will they let the giants they encounter deter them from their goals? Or will they courageously face them head on?

There is another parallel to this story. It is of Moses and the people of Israel standing on the edge of the Promised Land. Ten of the spies see the giants and are deterred from claiming God's Promised Land. Only Joshua and Caleb are willing to face the giants. Congregations also face giants and must make decisions about how to deal with them.

Sermon Starter Two

Do you believe in giants? (You may want to insert personal examples of your experience with giant challenges in your life. The following are some examples of giant challenges.)

It seems I've dealt with giants my whole life! The first giant I recall was when I was in the eighth grade. It was the giant of learning algebra. I was an excellent student, that is, up to this eighth-grade math class. Yes, it was a giant and I had to deal with it by working hard to get those basic concepts. I recall another giant that appeared the next year disguised in the form of a cute young schoolmate. The giant of fear seized me in a most serious way. I was virtually dumbstruck as I tried to get up the courage to ask my classmate to the school dance. But I had to face it. I'm glad I did because she turned out to be my first date.

We do encounter giants all through our lives. The question is how we will deal with them. Will we let them deter us from our goals? Will we run from the giants, or will we have the courage to meet them head on? Moses and the people of Israel stood on the edge of the Promised Land. Ten of the spies saw that there were giants in the land, and it deterred them from claiming God's Promised Land. Only Joshua and Caleb were willing to face the giants. Every church faces giants throughout its life. The question is, how will the congregation choose to deal with these giants?

Week Four: Asking the Right Questions
Mark 9:30-35

Introduction

Faithful questions invite us to engage in dialogue that leads to a realization of where to find true power. Genesis 3:9 records that God's first words to Adam and Eve, following their choice to eat from the tree of the knowledge of good and evil, were in the form of a question: "Where are you?" This sermon centers on the understanding that the true power of God is realized through the asking of right and faithful questions.

Mark 9:30-35 provides the focal point of the sermon as Jesus engages his disciples to understand where to find true power as he asks the question, "What were you arguing about on the way?" (This verse can also be translated, "What were you discussing on the way?") Jesus asks this question because he realizes the disciples have been asking the wrong question. Their question was about who was the greatest among them. This question did not invite dialogue as the disciples engaged in a power struggle. In response, Jesus taught the disciples about where to find true power: "Whoever wants to be first must be last of all and servant of all."

This sermon invites people to think about the questions they are asking through their lives and through their church. This invitation will lead them to consider where they may find true power as they understand Jesus as the Savior who became the last of all and servant of all through the cross.

Points to Consider

Point One: Right questions of faith are reflective and seek understanding, and they center on holy conversation and conferencing rather than debate and accusation. Right questions of faith confront us with the right questions about our lives. Some of the right questions in the Gospel of Mark are:

> What were you discussing on the way? (Mark 9:33)

> Who do you say that I am? (Mark 8:29)

Point Two: Faith in Jesus Christ invites disciples of Jesus to ask right questions about themselves as well as right questions about their communities of faith. Some of the right questions that faith in Jesus invites disciples to ask are:

- What have we been discussing on the way?
- Where do we find power in our lives as disciples of Jesus?
- How does our community of faith witness to who we say Jesus is?
- What are the right questions we should be asking?

Point Three: Jesus asked the right question of his disciples when they were engaged in a power struggle about who was the greatest among them. Rather than becoming ensnared in a debate about power, Jesus engaged in conversation that invited the disciples to understand where they could find true power in their lives:

> But they were silent, for on the way they had argued with one another about who was the greatest. He sat down, called the

twelve, and said to them, "Whoever wants to be first must be last of all and servant of all" (Mark 9:34-35).

Point Four: Faith in Jesus Christ invites disciples of Jesus to understand that their Savior revealed the true power of God as Jesus became least of all and servant of all through the cross and the resurrection. In the questions Jesus asked and in the lessons Jesus taught, we find the true power of Jesus in the cross because it is on the cross that Jesus' true identity is understood:

> They went on from there and passed through Galilee. He did not want anyone to know it; for he was teaching his disciples, saying to them, "The Son of Man is to be betrayed into human hands, and they will kill him, and three days after being killed, he will rise again" (Mark 9:31-32).

Point Five: Faith in Jesus Christ invites his disciples to live in God's power by becoming the least of all and the servant of all as they understand the questions they are asking as well as the questions other people are asking. Disciples of Jesus understand they must listen carefully and understand the questions they are asking because their intent resides in their questions. They are mindful of where true power resides as they define their identities and their ministries through Jesus' questions for their lives.

Possible Sermon Starters

SERMON STARTER ONE

Parents can attest to the importance of learning how to ask their children the right questions. If you want to learn about a child's day at school you can't ask, "How was your day" because it's too easy for the child to simply respond with (let the congregation respond) "Fine." By the way, did you know that the word *fine* is sometimes used as an acronym? I've heard that "Fine" as an acronym actually means Frenetic, Insecure, Neurotic and Exasperated!

We learn quickly that to actually find out about our child's day we must ask open-ended questions that invite conversation. Questions like, "Tell me about your day" or "What was the topic of your English literature class today" open dialogue. Close-ended questions will typically only get us one-word responses like *fine*, *good*, *okay*, etc. These quickly end our attempt to engage in conversation. Asking the right questions is not only important as we talk with our children; it is also important if we wish to engage in conversation with one another. Being aware of asking the right questions and hearing the questions being asked of us can be very instructive.

Jesus teaches us how to ask the right questions and in so doing shows us where we may find true power.

Sermon Starter Two

Have a question? Just Google it. This is a familiar refrain these days. What did we do before Google? I think we used books! Of course, there are all types of questions. There are questions that lead us to knowledge of a discipline or that provide facts and figures. There are questions that provide directions, instruction, protection, even joy. Some questions serve to build relationships. Some questions become accusations. Some questions help a cause; other questions tend to be divisive. Asking questions is an important part of our daily life.

In the Gospel of Mark, Jesus teaches about the importance of asking the "right questions" and in so doing gives us insight into where to find true power.

Week Five Sermon: Beyond and Within
Mark 8:34-37

Introduction

Mark 8:34-37 contains an invitation to discipleship that was beyond the past and present contexts of the disciples' lives. Until this point, Jesus' disciples had followed Jesus' invitation to be fishers of people as detailed in Mark 1:14-20. This invitation to discipleship had led to success that was beyond the world's wisdom. The sick had been healed, unclean spirits had been driven out of people's lives, and the kingdom of God had been revealed through the preaching and teaching of Jesus. New life had been given to the dead, the hungry had been fed, and Jesus had walked on water.

Jesus could tell, however, that the past and present successes of his first invitation to discipleship were not going to reveal the full extent of God's kingdom. There was only one way that could be done: Calvary. Assessing the current reality of his ministry, Jesus extended a second invitation to discipleship that envisioned a life that was beyond his disciples' current understanding of reality. A biblical principle called *Beyond and Within* defines this second invitation to discipleship.

Beyond and Within teaches that the current reality of discipleship is always assessed through the transforming truth of the cross of Jesus. This invitation to discipleship mandates that the vision of discipleship must be beyond self-focused concerns as Jesus' followers take up their cross and lose their lives for Jesus' sake and the gospel's. If present values that hinder people from living into a new identity as followers of Jesus define current reality, then people must intentionally choose a vision of life that transforms present values. *Beyond and Within* is an invitation to discipleship that is beyond the current reality of life.

Points to Consider

Point One: The time had arrived for Jesus to assess the current reality of discipleship. Measured by the world's standards, Jesus' first invitation to discipleship, defined in Mark 1:14-20 as being fishers of people, had a high success rate. Jesus understood, however, that faithful discipleship is measured by a different standard than the world's definition of success. With this understanding, Jesus issued a second invitation for his disciples to follow him in Mark 8:34-37:

> He called the crowd with his disciples, and said to them, "If any want to become my followers, let them deny themselves and take up their cross and follow me. For those who want to save their life will lose it, and those who lose their life for my sake, and for the sake of the gospel, will save it. For what will it profit them to gain the whole world and forfeit their life? Indeed, what can they give in return for their life?"

Point Two: A biblical principle called *Beyond and Within*. Defines Jesus' second invitation to discipleship. *Beyond and Within* teaches that the current reality of discipleship is always assessed through the transforming truth of the cross of Jesus. This invitation to discipleship mandates that the vision of discipleship must be beyond self-focused concerns as Jesus' followers take up their cross and lose their lives for Jesus' sake and the gospel's. An invitation to discipleship that is beyond the current reality of life, this invitation teaches that intentional choices must be made for a vision of life that transforms present values.

Point Three: Just as is true for an individual disciple's life, communities of Jesus' disciples must live by the principle of *Beyond and Within* if they wish to be transformed. Congregations that live by the biblical principle of *Beyond and Within* realize that if they want to live in the vision of the risen Christ they must first look to the cross of the crucified Christ. The goal for ministry within these congregations is to nurture and equip people to live as Jesus' disciples as the present values of their lives are transformed for Jesus' sake and for the gospel's. Churches that apply this biblical teaching assess the current reality of their ministry by how they are nurturing people to be disciples of Jesus as they equip them to see beyond their self-focused concerns. Remembering Jesus' admonition to lose their lives for Jesus' sake and the gospel's, they share the love of God by focusing beyond their own concerns. Through this same self-giving vision, they also look within at those things that are hindering them from living as God's called people. Following Jesus' sacrificial example of love, they are transformed by the cross of Jesus. Congregations that are transformed by the biblical principal of Jesus' second invitation to discipleship understand that the resurrection of a new day for ministry is possible only through the cross of Jesus Christ. They understand that an honest assessment of the present reality of ministry may require a new vision for ministry that is beyond all that has led to their past or present successes.

Point Four: A vision that invites people to look beyond their self-focused concerns defines effective ministry in churches that are bound for the Promised Land of discipleship. Remembering Jesus' admonition to take up their cross, they share the love of God by focusing on the sending love of God that led Jesus to the cross. Transformed by the cross of Jesus Christ, they look within their community of faith at those things that are hindering them from living as God's called people. Understanding that the context of following Jesus to Calvary and the empty tomb frames Jesus' invitation to the cross, they know that the journey of discipleship is always a journey beyond the present context of their church's life. Realizing that Jesus' crucifixion and resurrection fully reveal the truth of God's kingdom, they have accepted Jesus' second invitation to discipleship.

Possible Sermon Starters

SERMON STARTER ONE

Last week we considered the teaching of Jesus about the importance of asking the right questions. We saw how our questions can give insight into our intentions. We were also reminded that true power, God's power, is found as we begin to claim Jesus' call to deny ourselves and seek to serve the least, the last, and the lost. Simply put, we have the choice either to focus on self to the exclusion of others or to serve others in the name of Jesus to glorify God. We must make the same decision as a church. Will we have a self-serving inward focus, or will we look beyond self to a world that desperately needs the sacred touch of God? Will the church be a relevant presence for Christ and the glory of God or will it choose to live a life of irrelevance?

A church needed a new facility because it was located in a fast-growing suburban community. The church found itself in a constant struggle to find space for worship and its new and expanding programs. Finally, a capital campaign was completed, a new site was secured, and construction began. Because of the many worshipers on Sunday morning, an expansive parking lot was needed. It was beautiful and inviting, but its appeal was not limited to Sunday-morning worshipers. It was also ideal for the many skateboarders in the adjacent neighborhoods. "What! Skateboarders on the new pavement! What are we to do?" cried the trustees. Would they put up no trespassing signs to dissuade the neighborhood youth? Would it be necessary to patrol the area during after-school hours? What were they going to do to protect their newly paved parking lots?

Enter a creative, retired, and lifelong athlete. He would talk with the youth and see what could be done. The conversations with the youth, and later with the trustees, resulted in a surprising turn of events. Rather than prohibiting the skateboarders from using the parking lot, the church embraced their presence and formed a weekly Bible study for them. Later, this ministry became a draw for other youth as it expanded to include monthly outings to "primo" skateboarding sites around the state. A youth ministry was born.

The church had a choice. They could focus inwardly, on themselves, and the protection of the beautiful and inviting new facility, or they could choose to use the beautiful and inviting new facility to nurture the faith of their neighbors. They made a decision to focus beyond themselves as they applied a biblical principle called *Beyond and Within*. We will begin by looking at Jesus' call to the disciples to take up their cross and follow him in the Gospel of Mark.

Sermon Starter Two

Consider a time when you had to make a lofty decision, a decision that you knew was right but that would require a change of attitude or behavior. It may have been going back to college as an adult. Perhaps it was changing your eating habits or a decision to start working out at the health club. In my life, I can think of lots of examples, and I'm sure you can as well.

What makes these changes so difficult? One reason is that changing established habits in your life is not easy. It takes time and determination. Another reason could be that the old behavior or attitude is simply easier than the better alternative. Another could be that our current habits were taught to us as children and have become almost instinctive. There are a myriad of reasons, but the bottom line is that some behaviors and attitudes have become the norm for each of us. It's just the way we are.

As we consider our faith, we also have challenges and decisions that must be made. We need to assess continually if our attitudes and behaviors are consistent with Christ's call to discipleship. If not, we will need to make changes. Some changes will undoubtedly require perseverance.

One of the fundamental decisions that we and the church must make is whether we and the church exist for ourselves or as a means to proclaim the gospel message. This understanding comes from the biblical principle of *Beyond and Within*. This biblical principle is best understood as we look in the Gospel of Mark as Jesus' call to the disciples to take up their cross and follow him.

Week Six Sermon: Entering God's Promised Land
Philippians 2:1-11

Introduction

If a congregation is going to enter God's Promised Land of discipleship, its members must intentionally choose to empty themselves of their own agendas as they take on the nature and mission of Jesus Christ. Rather than being driven by the human need to win, the redeemed need to serve leads them. Singing the redeeming song of God's faithfulness, congregations transform through the power of Christ's servant nature. This unified song of redemption is not easy to learn or sing. It requires members of a congregation to define their lives by humility as they look out for the interests of others. Rather than seeking the self-preservation of personal interests, members of a transformed congregation understand that self-emptying love defines their responses to Christian discipleship. Instead of being a collection of dissonant voices that seek to preserve cherished memories of the past or cherished ministries of the present, a transformed congregation looks beyond itself to the power of the cross of Jesus Christ. Singing in the harmony of servant faith, a congregation is transformed when its members have the mind of Christ among them.

This sermon encourages a church to enter God's Promised Land of discipleship as defined by the apostle Paul in Philippians 2:1-4. It challenges a church to enter this Promised Land by affirming the self-emptying love that empowered Jesus to become the least of all and the servant of all through the cross as defined by the "kenosis hymn" (a Greek word that means self-emptying) in Philippians 2:5-11. The words of this song of praise witness to the deliberate choices of self-emptying love that defined the nature of Jesus as he walked the path of the cross. Paul, the author of the Letter to the Philippians, models this self-giving love as he gives thanks for this congregation.

Points to Consider

Point One: Your community of faith can enter God's Promised Land for Jesus' disciples. Your church has a prayer for living in the envisioned reality that Paul described for the church in Philippians 2:1-4:

> If then there is any encouragement in Christ, any consolation from love, any sharing in the Spirit, any compassion and sympathy, make my joy complete: be of the same mind, having the same love, being in full accord and of one mind. Do nothing from selfish ambition or conceit, but in humility regard others as better than yourselves. Let each of you look not to your own interests, but to the interests of others.

Point Two: To live in the envisioned reality of Philippians 2:1-4, churches must make intentional choices of faith that empower Jesus' disciples to live in the same self-giving love that guided Jesus to the cross. Philippians 2:5-11 defines this self-giving or self-emptying love:

> Let the same mind be in you that was in Christ Jesus, who, though he was in the form of God, did not regard equality with God as something to be exploited, but emptied himself, taking the form of a slave, being born in human likeness. And being found in human form, he humbled himself and became obedient to the point of death—even death on a cross. Therefore God also highly exalted him and gave him the name that is above every name, so that at the name of Jesus every knee should bend, in heaven and on earth and under the earth, and every tongue should confess that Jesus Christ is Lord, to the glory of God the Father.

Point Three: Paul demonstrated this self-giving love as he wrote his letter to the Philippians. Writing from a prison cell because of his witness of faith, Paul was able to rejoice and be thankful because he had entered God's Promised Land for Jesus' disciples. Paul glorified God because his life had become a song of faith to Jesus. He rejoiced and was thankful because he had become the servant of all as he followed Jesus in the call of discipleship that leads to the cross of Calvary and to the reality of the empty tomb. It was the reality of the servant ministry of Christ that Paul envisioned as he wrote to the Philippians about doing nothing from selfishness or conceit, in humility counting others better than themselves, looking not only to their own interests, but also to the interests of others.

Point Four: All disciples of Jesus can demonstrate the self-giving love of

Jesus. They can live into the joy and unity of Jesus' prayer for his disciples in John 17. This vision defined by Jesus' prayer for his disciples can become their vision as they share their faith through the life of their congregation. United through faith in Jesus, communities of Jesus' disciples can fulfill the mission of Jesus' prayer by living as God's people sent into the world so that the world may believe that God sent Jesus.

Point Five: All congregations must make intentional decisions about their nature and mission if they wish to demonstrate the self-giving love of Jesus. Congregations that choose to have their nature and mission defined by Philippians 2:1-4 will need to determine what is hindering them from entering this Promised Land of discipleship by asking the right questions that lead to faith in Jesus. Having asked these questions, they must then have the mind of Christ among them defined by Philippians 2:5-11 as they live in an envisioned reality that glorifies God by allowing the self-emptying love of Jesus to guide the focus of their life together.

Possible Sermon Starters

SERMON STARTER ONE

One of the great pleasures of being a pastor is the privilege of visiting a couple immediately following the birth of their first child. Joy and excitement abound as the new parents begin to care for their newborn and introduce him or her to their friends and family. It is not unusual, however, for the joy and excitement to turn into a bit of anxiety after going home. The shock of this responsibility can be overwhelming as they come face to face with the reality that life is no longer solely about their wants and needs. In just a matter of a few days, they have been moved to second place on the hierarchy of importance. Now they are asked to give of themselves for a much greater cause: the cause of new life.

As we accept a new life in Christ, the reality of discipleship can be equally shocking. Although we do not have a newborn as a daily reminder of the nature of our call, our call is no less demanding. Jesus was crystal clear that the role of a disciple extends beyond self. It is most clearly demonstrated as we look toward the cross of Calvary and at Jesus washing the feet of his disciples on the night before his crucifixion.

SERMON STARTER TWO

We have waited years for this to happen. Many months have gone into the planning. We have orchestrated the travel. We know the route. We have poured over what has been written about our adventure and have an idea of what to expect when we arrive. It promises to be an experience like no other. We can barely contain our excitement and expectation. We will never sleep tonight because tomorrow is the day . . . tomorrow is the day . . . the day we depart for the majesty of Disneyworld! Can you relate?

For over four hundred years the Israelites anticipated entering the land promised to Abraham, God's Promised Land. Imagine how they must have felt as they looked over into the land of Canaan. It was a land of milk and honey. Could they even imagine what it would it be like living in God's Promised Land? How about you? Can you imagine what God's Promised Land looks like for you and for our church today?

APPENDIX 3

Synopsis of Bible Studies

The Bible study that accompanies this Leader's Guide is an intentional process of spiritual engagement for your church. Through this study, your congregation will learn to speak the same biblical language as it learns about God's Promised Land for disciples of Jesus. In learning this language, members will hear how the story of the twelve spies who presented a report about God's Promised Land to the congregation of Israel also tells the story of today's church. Learning this story, they will identify the giants that are dwelling in the Promised Land God has envisioned for your community of faith and understand where to find true power as they ask and answer right questions about your congregation. Your church will learn how the biblical principle of *Beyond and Within* can transform the identity of a congregation and discover why it is essential for members of a congregation to have the mind of Christ among them if they wish to enter God's Promised Land for Jesus' disciples.

Bible-study participants will also respond to questions that will formulate information about the current reality of your church. These responses, in turn, will allow your church to make intentional decisions about the nature and mission of your life together as your congregation discerns its strategic-ministry plan. The following synopsis provides the basic understandings and key concepts of each Bible study that will provide the foundation for your church's vision and mission as a community of faith.

Bible Study One: Does Your Church Have a Prayer?
Scripture: John 17:1-26

Foundational Understanding

John 17 records Jesus' prayer for communities of Jesus' disciples who stand on the edge of God's Promised Land.

Key Concepts

Understanding that Jesus' call to discipleship is an invitation to join in God's story of salvation, disciples of Jesus answer their Savior's call upon their lives. They understand that living in God's Promised Land of discipleship is possible only as they live as communities of faith in the vision of Jesus' prayer for them.

Followers of Jesus have one purpose for their life and ministry: to glorify God. Jesus prayed for this as he focused beyond his own concerns to the concerns of his followers.

Focusing beyond themselves, Christian disciples honor God when they understand themselves as people sent into the world by Jesus. By acts of faithfulness that point beyond their own concerns, congregations of disciples can become transforming symbols of God's presence to people who are searching for purpose in their lives. God's Promised Land of discipleship occurs as Jesus' followers live in the unity of community with each other. The corporate life of the Church nurtures and equips disciples of Jesus Christ to live out the nature and mission of Jesus' visionary prayer.

Key Scriptural Points

Sanctification is the vision of Jesus' prayer for his disciples in John 17:17-19: "Sanctify them in the truth; your word is truth. As you have sent me into the world, so I have sent them into the world. And for their sakes I sanctify myself, so that they also may be sanctified in truth." An act of God's searching and sending grace, sanctification describes the nature of God's Promised Land for Jesus' disciples. In this Promised Land, Jesus' disciples are empowered to look beyond themselves and live as people who are sent into the world through the power of God's love. It is through sanctification that followers of Jesus grow and mature in their faith as the Spirit forms them into the image of Christ.

Joy and unity are the milk and honey of God's Promised Land for Jesus' disciples. These qualities define the nature of Jesus' disciples when the Spirit forms them into the image of Christ. In 17:13, Jesus prayed for joy for his disciples: "But now I am coming to you, and I speak these things in the world so that they may have my joy made complete in themselves." In 17:22-23, Jesus prayed for unity for his disciples as they lived the message of God's love he had been sent to share: "The glory that you have given me I have given them, so that they may be one, as we are one, I in them and you in me, that they may become completely one, so that the world may know that you have sent me and have loved them even as you have loved me."

Love in the Christian community is a calling beyond self-focus. The first fruit of the Holy Spirit listed in Galatians 5:21, love bears witness to the "sending" power of God through Jesus. As churches live in the "sending" power of God's love, they are united through a divine vision of the cross that calls them to a communal life beyond the pettiness and grumblings that can sometimes dominate the culture of a congregation. This divine vision leads to intentional ministry where a sense of mission and hope defines the spirit of the congregation.

The communal life of congregations bound for God's Promised Land is defined by missional qualities as their members are challenged to focus beyond themselves by:

- Glorifying God through their faith in Jesus (17:10): "All mine are yours, and yours are mine; and I have been glorified in them."

- Understanding their call as people who are sent into the world (17:18): "As you have sent me into the world, so I have sent them into the world."

- Making God's love known through Jesus (17:26): "I made your name known to them, and I will make it known, so that the love with which you have loved me may be in them, and I in them."

Bible Study Two: What Reality Do You Choose?
Scripture: Numbers 13:1–14:9

Foundational Understanding

Numbers 13:1-14:9 is an analogy of today's Church as it stands on the edge of the Promised Land Jesus envisioned for his disciples in John 17.

Key Concepts

Reality is the present experience of life. Numbers 13:1-14:9 teaches that we can interpret reality in two ways. Perceived reality is allowing your perceptions of past experiences and your subsequent fears of the future to control your responses to the present. Envisioned reality is allowing God's promised future to control your responses to the present.

Our vision and interpretation of reality can allow us to enter God's Promised Land for Jesus' disciples or cause us to wander in the wilderness as we cling to the past. Either a local church's ministry can be the present fulfillment of God's promises, or it can cause wandering in the wilderness of murmuring. To face the present challenges of ministry, a local church must have an understanding of the Promised Land God has envisioned for disciples of Jesus Christ.

A local church must answer the following question as it plans its ministries: will it plan its ministries based on memories of the past, or will it plan its ministries as the church is formed by the promises of Jesus Christ? The answer to this question will determine whether a church lives in perceived reality or envisioned reality. Will it allow the perceptions of the past to control the church's response to the giants that are facing its future ministry, or will it allow the promise of God's presence in the future to guide the vision of the church's present ministry?

We experience God's judgment when God allows us to live in the reality of our fearful and untrusting vision of life. We experience God's grace as we live with trust in the promise of God's presence and vision for the future.

Key Scriptural Points

We find the perceived reality that controlled the response of the ten spies and the congregation of Israel in Numbers 13:33: "to ourselves we seemed like grasshoppers, and so we seemed to them." Reporting on the reality of giants in the Promised Land, the ten spies' interpretation of reality reflected how the spies perceived themselves as they faced the challenge of the giants who dwelled in the Promised Land. Feeling inadequate to meet the challenge that was before them, they began to focus on the inadequacy of their own self-perceptions rather than on the promised future that God had given to Abraham. These spies' vision of the future could not see beyond the present reality of the giants who dwelled in the Promised Land, nor could their vision see beyond themselves. As a result, the spies' present perception of seeming like grasshoppers to the giants and to themselves controlled their response to the future that God had promised them.

We find the envisioned reality that controlled the response of Joshua and Caleb in Numbers 14:7-9:

> "The land that we went through as spies is an exceedingly good land. If the LORD is pleased with us, he will bring us into this land and give it to us, a land that flows with milk and honey. Only, do not rebel against the LORD; and do not fear the people of the land, for they are no more than bread for us; their protection is removed from them, and the LORD is with us; do not fear them."

Guided by God's promised vision of the future, these two spies challenged the congregation of Israel to trust in God's present and future faithfulness.

Jesus' disciples experience the reality of God's Promsed Land as they trust in the promise and vision of Jesus' prayer in John 17. The nature of this Promised Land is a church where Jesus' disciples are made complete in his joy, sanctified in the truth of God, and united as Jesus and his "Heavenly Father" are one. Members glorifying God through their faith, understanding their call as people sent into the world, and making God's love known through Jesus define the ministry of congregations in this Promised Land.

Bible Study Three: Overcoming Giants
Scripture: Numbers 13:25–14:9

Foundational Understanding

All Promised Lands have giants dwelling in them. In order to overcome the general and specific giants that a congregation faces, it must allow its vision to focus beyond the fearful reality of giants. This will happen only as the congregation focuses on living as people sent into the world through the power of God's love. Blessed by joy and unity, congregations that overcome the giants that face them live as communities of Jesus' disciples who glorify God by their very existence.

Key Concepts

Every local congregation stands on the edge of God's Promised Land that Jesus envisioned in his prayer for his disciples almost two thousand years ago. In the hope of this prayer, God intervened on behalf of Jesus' disciples through the life, death, and resurrection of Jesus, delivering them from the slavery of sin and death into the hope of a new day.

The context of the congregation of Israel applies to the context of your congregation. The congregation of Israel was standing on the edge of the promise God had made to Abraham. The hope of this Promised Land resided in God's faithfulness. Like Israel's trust in the promise of God's faithfulness, the hope of the Promised Land for Jesus' disciples resides in God's faithfulness through Jesus. The congregation of Israel had to choose how they would respond to the general and specific giants that were dwelling in the Promised Land, either by focusing their vision on the empowering promise of God's faithfulness, or by focusing their vision on their self-limiting perceptions of themselves. Local congregations have the same choices to make as they respond to the reality of giants that dwell in God's Promised Land for Jesus' disciples.

There are three general giants facing the church as modern culture searches for a sense of direction. The first general giant is the giant of worldviews. Within the wilderness of our modern society, people are searching as they struggle with worldviews. They are asking what they must do to survive. In the midst of this wilderness, God calls the church to help people understand there is a God who cares about them and their world.

The second general giant is the giant of technology. While technology will determine the methods by which we communicate the Good News, it is important to realize that society does not define the message of Jesus Christ. That message is the same yesterday, today, and forever (Hebrews 13:8). It is also essential to realize this eternal message presents the church with the possibility for reaching people at a level of interaction that technology alone will not achieve: the need to be connected to God's sacred touch. It is the sacred story of God's sacred touch that gives the church the power and authority to speak to a meaning of life that is beyond human knowledge.

The third general giant facing the church is the giant of expectation. Advances in technology create this giant when people expect new and improved methods to make their lives more controllable. As people live in pursuit of this expectation, they realize their search for excellence does not satisfy the human need for God's presence in life. Realizing that the giant of expectation cannot meet the deepest needs of life, people search for meaning as they deal with the challenges of life in today's world. This search for meaning presents the church with the holy responsibility of connecting people to the eternal story of God's love in Jesus Christ. To accept this challenge, a congregation must equip itself for a new day of ministry as it connects people with the eternal message of God's love in ways that are relevant to the present challenges of life. This will happen as the church helps people to envision a life that is beyond their expectations.

Every local church has specific giants that it faces in the context of its ministry setting. Some of these giants may be a congregation with a history of conflict, a congregation that limits its leadership base to a few selected members who maintain or exchange the same offices within the church, a congregation that does not reflect the diversity of its changing neighborhood, an aging facility, a congregation of limited resources, etc. Over time, the specific giants can take on mythical proportions as they shape and control the culture and structure of a congregation. When allowed, specific giants can cause members to focus on institutional survival rather than to look beyond themselves as missional expressions of God's Holy Spirit. Instead of living as people guided by

God's promise of faithfulness for Jesus' disciples, self-perceptions control these congregations.

Key Scriptural Points

The story of God's sacred touch upon human life is the story of the Bible. Genesis 2:7 tells of how "the LORD God formed man from the dust of the ground, and breathed into his nostrils the breath of life; and the man became a living being." Genesis 3 tells the repeating story of how humanity chooses to live outside of a trusting relationship with God, who breathes life into our very existence. From this original sin emerges the remaining story of the Bible. It is the story of a God who continually reaches out to a creation that has fallen from God's spoken goodness, a creation defined by a humanity whose image is blurred by mistrust and willful self-interests. It is the story of God's Word becoming flesh and dwelling among humanity "full of grace and truth" (John 1:14). Paul writes of how God's saving acts through Jesus allow Gentiles to participate in the promise of God's faithfulness to Abraham: "Christ redeemed us from the curse of the law by becoming a curse for us—for it is written, 'Cursed is everyone who hangs on a tree'—in order that in Christ Jesus the blessing of Abraham might come to the Gentiles, so that we might receive the promise of the Spirit through faith" (Galatians 3:13-14). The hope of this redemption resides in God's faithfulness through Jesus. Ultimately, the story of the Bible is the redemptive story of God's sacred touch being restored with humankind through a new heaven and a new earth as God wipes "every tear from their eyes" (Revelation 21:4).

Bible Study Four: Asking the Right Questions
Scripture: Mark 9:30-35

Foundational Understanding

Where do we find true power? The Gospel of Mark invites you to answer this question by asking the right questions as you walk on the path of discipleship that leads to the cross and empty tomb of Jesus. On this path, you must answer questions that Jesus asks all of his disciples, questions such as, "What were you discussing on the way?" and "Who do you say that I am?" Your answers to these questions will say much about where you may find true power in your life and in the life of your church.

Key Concepts

The reason we must listen carefully and understand the questions we are asking is because our intent resides in our questions. When we experience tension
or conflict in the life of a church or in the lives of people, it is essential to
understand the context in which people ask questions. Right questions invite
dialogue, understanding, and strengthening of community and relationship.
Wrong questions invite accusation, labeling, and destruction of community
and relationship.

When power struggles confront us, we need to remember where true
power resides as we define our identities and our ministries through Jesus'
calling upon our lives. One of the sad realities churches face is that some people or groups would rather watch a congregation become less effective in ministry, decline, and sometimes die because they do not want to give up their
power. When congregations are willing to die as they struggle with the world's
definition of power rather than live in the power of the cross, the question they
need to ask is if they are willing to let go of their power struggles for Jesus'
sake and the gospel's. The cross of Jesus Christ asks every congregation what it
values most as that congregation answers the question Jesus asks of his disciples: "Who do you say that I am?"

The empty tomb of Jesus Christ invites Jesus' disciples to live in a new
understanding of power as they ask the question, "Who will roll away the
stone from the door of the tomb for us?" Easter is Jesus' invitation to live in
the victory of Calvary and to follow Jesus as the risen Christ by living a life
that has a future. The good news of the empty tomb is that God offers followers of Jesus resurrected possibilities of life through a future they have not yet
experienced. It is a powerful invitation, a frightening invitation, an invitation
to take up the cross and live by losing our lives for the sake of Jesus and the
gospel.

Key Scriptural Points

Where do we find true power? To arrive at the answer to these questions, it is
essential to consider the first and last questions recorded in Mark. The initial
question recorded in Mark is by an unclean spirit in Mark 1:24: "What have
you to do with me, Jesus of Nazareth? Have you come to destroy us?" The con-
frontation does not conclude with these questions as the unclean spirit states,
"I know who you are, the Holy One of God." Rather than simply stating Jesus'
identity, the unclean spirit is attempting to limit Jesus' identity by engaging
Jesus in a power struggle. Jesus would not allow the destructive questions of
the unclean spirit to limit his identity. The Holy One of God was not going to
allow the wrong questions to define his ministry. Jesus' ministry was about

redemption rather than destruction. Rather than allowing himself to become possessed by a power struggle with the unclean spirit, Jesus commanded the spirit to "be silent and come out of him!" (Mark 1:25).

The last question asked in Mark occurs on Easter morning in Mark 16:3. Going to the tomb to anoint the crucified Jesus, Mary Magdalene, Mary the mother of James, and Salome ask each other, "Who will roll away the stone for us from the entrance to the tomb?" Following this question, Mark 16:4-7 records, "When they looked up, they saw that the stone, which was very large, had already been rolled back. As they entered the tomb, they saw a young man, dressed in a white robe, sitting on the right side; and they were alarmed. But he said to them, 'Do not be alarmed; you are looking for Jesus of Nazareth, who was crucified. He has been raised; he is not here. Look, there is the place they laid him. But go, tell his disciples and Peter that he is going ahead of you to Galilee; there you will see him, just as he told you.'" Jesus' disciples have the mission of living in a new understanding of power, the Easter power of the crucified and resurrected Jesus Christ.

How are Jesus' disciples defined? We find the answer to this question in the right questions Jesus asks all of his disciples: "What were you discussing on the way?" and "Who do you say that I am?" Jesus' disciples define their identity by how they answer the right question Jesus asked in Mark 9:33 as his disciples engaged in a power struggle over who was the greatest among them: "Then they came to Capernaum; and when he was in the house he asked them, "What were you discussing on the way?" Jesus' disciples answer this question as they accept Jesus' invitation to live in the victory of Calvary and follow him as the risen Christ by living a life that has a future. After asking this question, Jesus taught about true power in Mark 9:35: "Whoever wants to be first must be last of all and servant of all." Disciples of Jesus define their identity by seeking to be last of all and servants of all.

Jesus' disciples also define their identity through the cross of Jesus. Mark records that Jesus began to teach about his crucifixion after Peter identified him as the Messiah when Jesus asked, "Who do you say that I am?" Mark 8:31-35 records Jesus' teaching about his impending crucifixion and resurrection with a second calling to discipleship: "If any want to become my followers, let them deny themselves and take up their cross and follow me. For those who want to save their life will lose it, and those who lose their life for my sake, and for the sake of the gospel, will save it." The journey of Christian discipleship leads to the cross of the crucified Jesus Christ before it leads to the empty tomb of the resurrected Jesus Christ. Jesus' disciples understand their true identity through the cross.

Bible Study Five: Beyond and Within
Scripture: Mark 1:16-20, Mark 8:34-37

Foundational Understanding

Beyond and Within is a scriptural foundation for churches that seek to share the love of God through an outward focus. Churches that apply this biblical teaching assess the current reality of their ministry by how they are inviting people to be disciples of Jesus. Remembering Jesus' admonition to lose their lives for Jesus' sake and the gospel's, they share the love of God by focusing beyond their own concerns. Through this same self-giving vision, they also look within at those things that are hindering them from living as God's called people. Following Jesus' sacrificial example of love, the cross of Jesus transforms them. They have accepted Jesus' second invitation to discipleship even though it means they may have to live into a new identity as they assess the current reality of their ministry.

Key Concepts

Jesus' call to discipleship is always an invitation for Jesus' disciples to follow their Savior as they live into a new identity. Jesus' first invitation to discipleship invited the disciples to become fishers of people. Jesus' second invitation to discipleship invited the disciples to become cross bearers.

The current reality of discipleship is always assessed through the transforming truth of the cross of Jesus. This invitation to discipleship mandates that the vision of discipleship must be beyond self-focused concerns as Jesus' followers take up their cross and lose their lives for Jesus' sake and the gospel's. If present values that hinder people from living into a new identity as followers of Jesus define current reality, then we must make intentional choices that transform present values.

Transformation occurs in churches that understand an honest assessment of the present reality of ministry may require a new vision for ministry that is beyond all that has led to their past or present successes. Rather than protecting cherished memories of the past or cherished ministries of the present, they focus their concerns on how they may share the gospel of Jesus Christ in the present reality of their ministry. They understand that the journey of discipleship is always a journey beyond the past and present contexts of their church's life.

Churches that allow their own needs to become the primary concern for their existence reverse the order of the biblical principle of *Beyond and Within* to "Within and Beyond." They allow their self-confining concerns to become the focus of their existence. Instead of allowing their ministry to focus beyond their own needs, they seek to save their lives. They face the challenges of the present by wandering in discouragement as they dwell on their past memories of success rather than envisioning possibilities of hope for their future. Sometimes these churches are chained to the cherished ministries of the present that focus energy on maintaining the comfort level within the congregation rather than allowing the congregation to look beyond. Whatever the reason, if an inward focus for ministry defines the existence of a congregation, then that congregation will become a symbol of irrelevance as it attempts to communicate with society God's message of grace through Jesus Christ. If a church's goal for ministry is to maintain its current successes or replicate past successes, then it will wander in the wilderness as it searches for a reason for its future existence.

Key Scriptural Points

Beyond and Within is the biblical order of Jesus' invitation to discipleship. Jesus calls his disciples to follow him in a journey that leads beyond the present as it transforms the present. The nature of Jesus' invitation to discipleship always challenges Jesus' disciples to live beyond the identity of their current reality. Mark 1:16-20 records Jesus' first invitation to discipleship as Jesus called Simon, Andrew, James, and John to become fishers of people. Mark 8:34-37 records Jesus' second invitation to discipleship as Jesus called his disciples to take up their cross and follow him.

Two portions of scripture that speak to the reason for the church's existence are the Great Commission of Matthew 28:16-20 and the Great Promise of Acts 1:8. Jesus gives the Great Commission of Matthew 28:16-20 at Galilee where he began his ministry. This home base for Jesus' earthly ministry becomes the launching point for Jesus' resurrected ministry as he commissions his disciples to answer a world-changing calling. The Great Commission teaches that the purpose of worship, teaching, and remembering is to strengthen the church's witness of focusing beyond itself as it goes and makes "disciples of all nations, baptizing them in the name of the Father and of the Son and of the Holy Spirit." The Great Promise of Acts 1:8 occurs at Bethany. Bethany was the village that served as the beginning point for Jesus' Palm Sunday entrance into Jerusalem. Riding on a donkey into the Holy City, Jesus taught about true power as he answered the call of being last of all and servant of all. It is at Bethany that the resurrected Jesus promises the power of God's kingdom to his disciples. The Great Promise teaches that the purpose of power from the Holy Spirit is for Jesus' disciples to be his "witnesses in Jerusalem and in all Judea and Samaria and to the end of the earth." In both the Great

Commission and the Great Promise, the envisioned reality of Jesus' disciples being called to a life of faith in a crucified and risen Lord defines the existence of the church.

Acts 6:1-7 is an example of the Jerusalem congregation transformed through the biblical principle of *Beyond and Within*. A concern had arisen because the Hellenist widows (Greek-speaking Jews or Jews who lived by Greek customs) were not being treated fairly in the daily distribution of food to the Hebrew widows (more conservative Jews). In response, the twelve apostles conducted a mission and ministry assessment that resulted in the congregation living by the biblical principle of *Beyond and Within*. The pressing ministry need of the Jerusalem congregation was equitable care for its members. The pressing mission of the Jerusalem congregation was the fulfillment of the Great Commission and the Great Promise. As the mission and ministry needs of the congregation met, a disagreement arose. Responding to this situation, the apostles modeled a pattern of resolution that is still applicable to today's congregations.

DEFINE THE MISSION OF THE CONGREGATION

The apostles clearly defined the mission of the Jerusalem congregation as they summoned the body of disciples and said, "It is not right that we should neglect the word of God in order to wait on tables." Clearly stating that the mission of the congregation was a call beyond internal needs, they created the context for resolution. They also determined that the internal needs of the congregation could not become the focus of the congregation's existence, nor could it become the focus of their ministry.

ASSESS CURRENT REALITY THROUGH MISSION VALUES

By assessing the current reality of the congregation through the mission value of preaching the word of God, the apostles determined that the congregation's internal needs could not be ignored while the mission of the congregation was being fulfilled.

ORGANIZE A RESPONSE THROUGH CONSULTATION WITH LEADERSHIP

Responding to the reality of the situation, the apostles organized a response by consulting with the leadership of the congregation in the selection of seven deacons who would oversee the internal needs that had become such a pressing issue. Following this time of mission definition, reality assessment, consultation, and organizing of a response, they reported their response to a congregation that was pleased with what they said.

ACHIEVE CONSENSUS BY THE CONGREGATION THAT WILL

ENABLE CURRENT REALITY TO BE TRANSFORMED

The result of this pattern of resolution was that the congregation maintained its focus on its reason for existence, its internal ministry needs were resolved, and the number of the disciples multiplied greatly. In other words, the current reality within the congregation was transformed as the identity of the congregation was defined through its stated mission.

Bible Study Six: Entering God's Promised Land
Scripture: Philippians 2:1-11

Foundational Understandings

If a congregation is going to enter God's Promised Land of discipleship, its members must intentionally choose to empty themselves of their own agendas as they take on the nature and mission of Jesus Christ. Rather than being driven by the human need to win, they are led by the redeemed need to serve. Singing the redeeming song of God's faithfulness, congregations transform through the power of Christ's servant nature. Just as the deliberate choices that empowered Jesus to take the form of a servant defined Jesus, the deliberate choices that will allow congregations to live in servant faith will define the identity of congregations bound for God's Promised Land. These congregations make intentional decisions about their nature and mission. These decisions are not top-down mandates from congregational leadership, nor are they momentary responses of emotions that are not connected to the overall vision of the congregation.

Congregations bound for God's Promised Land for Jesus' disciples ask the right questions: questions about Christian discipleship, questions about the nature and mission of a local congregation, questions about giants that are facing a congregation, questions about servant ministry as a congregation focuses beyond itself, and questions about the power of the cross of Jesus. As members of a congregation hear the right questions, they are able to discern and move toward the same vision of discipleship. This happens as they encourage one another and participate as a community of faith united by God's Holy Spirit. In turn, as the mind of Christ defines the nature and mission of a congregation, people beyond the congregation will begin asking questions about the transformation they see occurring. These questions will draw them to the power of God they are witnessing through the congregation's ministry.

Congregations bound for God's Promised Land for Jesus' disciples realize that the mind of Christ calls them to transformation. Acknowledging cherished memories of the past and cherished ministries of the present enables them to respect the present reality of their faith while focusing beyond the present into God's envisioned reality. Recognizing that ministry choices that led to their present maturity will likely cause them to plateau and begin a stage of decline in their life cycle, their leaders and members consult and create new expressions of ministry that define the mind of Christ among them. Focusing on the interests of others, they look beyond their own interests as they intentionally end those things that keep them from growing in their mission of witnessing to the grace of God in Jesus Christ.

All congregations must make intentional decisions about their nature and mission. Congregations bound for God's Promised Land for Jesus' disciples require consensus as people engaged in the discipline of hearing the same message and asking the same questions. In faithful conversations where the congregation determines its primary mission. They realize if they are to see with the vision of the risen Christ, they must first look to the cross of the crucified Christ. In doing this, they will live and relate with each other and their surrounding communities in an envisioned reality that glorifies God.

Key Scriptural Points

Your church has a prayer for living in the envisioned reality that Paul described for the church in Philippians 2:1-4, a reality defined by people doing nothing from selfishness or conceit, in humility counting others better than themselves, looking not only to their own interests, but also to the interests of others. To help the members of the church at Philippi understand how they could live in the reality of God's Promised Land of discipleship, Paul followed his words about the envisioned reality of Philippians 2:1-4 with the words of one of the ancient songs of Christianity in Philippians 2:5-11. This ancient praise of God affirms the self-emptying love that empowered Jesus to become the least of all and the servant of all through the cross. Known as the "kenosis hymn" (a Greek word that means self-emptying), the words of this song of praise witness to the deliberate choices of self-emptying love that define the nature of Jesus as he walked the path of the cross. As important as the words of the "kenosis hymn" are in understanding the nature of Jesus, they are equally important in understanding the nature of Christ's body.

The story of Pentecost is an example of what happens when people sing the song of God's faithfulness through Jesus. This story of the beginning of the church is told in Acts 2 as the disciples, empowered by the Holy Spirit, become apostles by proclaiming the message of God's grace they had witnessed through the life, death, and resurrection of Jesus. As the Holy Spirit danced like wildfire upon the apostles, they began to speak in the languages of people from around the world. This miraculous event signaled the birth of the church. The defining miracle of the church's birth, however, was not that the apostles were able to speak in languages they did not know. The defining miracle of the church's birth was that people from every nation around the world heard the same message of God's grace through Jesus. Upon hearing this message, they, in turn, asked the same question, "What does this mean," as they were drawn to the story of God's love through Jesus. As a result of the same message of God's grace being heard and trusted, the closing verse of Acts 2 records the following: "And day by day the Lord added to their number those who were being saved" (Acts 2:47).

Acts 15 tells one story of how the congregation in Jerusalem defined its nature and mission when a meeting known as the Jerusalem Council determined how it should recognize Gentiles as disciples of Jesus. The council decided that Gentile Christians would not have to observe the customs and requirements of Judaism. It also decided that Gentile Christians, out of respect for Jewish Christians, should live into their new nature as disciples of Jesus by abstaining from idols, from unchastity, from eating what is strangled, and from blood. Both the Jewish and Gentile Christians lived in the self-emptying love of Jesus as they looked beyond their own interests to the mission of the gospel of Jesus Christ. Entering God's Promised Land for disciples of Jesus, they put an end to what hindered them from looking to the interests of others, continued what gave foundation to their faith, and created new expressions of mission and ministry that defined the mind of Christ that was among them. Both Jewish and Gentile disciples looked beyond their own concerns and allowed the cross of Jesus Christ to define their corporate mission. Together, they achieved a response that transformed their mission of witnessing to the grace of God as they had the mind of Christ among them. Their faithfulness to this mission allowed them to move beyond conflict resolution to transformation.

Following the model of the Jerusalem Council, congregations bound for God's Promised Land of discipleship are able to move beyond concerns that hinder them from looking to the interests of others, to continue what gives foundation to their faith, and to create new expressions of mission and ministry that define the mind of Christ that is among them. They realize that if they are to see with the vision of the risen Christ, they must first look to the cross of the crucified Christ's self-emptying love. In doing this, they will live and relate with each other and their surrounding communities in an envisioned reality that glorifies God as they enter God's Promised Land for Jesus' disciples.

Strategic-Ministry Plan Covenant Card

John 17 includes Jesus' prayer for his followers. Our church will begin a process of study and listening that will help us to understand more fully how we can live in the vision and mission of Jesus' prayer. To assist in this process, a strategic-ministry plan task force has been approved. Your support is important in helping the task force to hear the voice of our church through your prayers, participation in small-group Bible study, and presentation of the plan for congregational feedback. As a sign of your support, please return this covenant card to the church office.

Believing that Jesus has prayed for his followers, I will:

_____ Pray for the my church daily;

_____ Pray for the Promised Land Task Force;

_____ Allow my voice to be heard by participating in a small-group Bible study;

_____ Attend worship regularly;

_____ Participate in the listening session when the task-force report is presented.

_____ Signature

APPENDIX 5

Covenant Prayer

Your Advance Leadership Team and the members of the Promised Land Task Force will affirm their commitment and participation by praying this prayer after signing their covenant card. It should also be used at the beginning of each PLTF meeting and the subsequent meetings led by the PLTF members.

> Holy God, you created us out of your love for humankind. It is out of your love for us that we have accepted your grace and chosen to follow Jesus, proclaiming the risen Christ. As Jesus' disciples, we know it is your desire for all the people of the world to be reconciled with you and one another for the redemption of all creation.

> We gather as your people now and give you thanks and praise for your presence in our lives. We give thanks for the ways in which you have guided and blessed this congregation. We seek your will and guidance. Holy God, we gather to listen and discern together as we covenant to follow Jesus for your glory. Amen.

Strategic-Ministry Plan Graphic

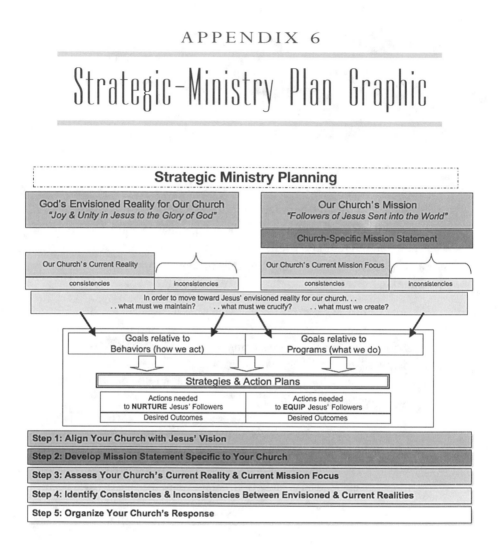

Strategic Ministry Planning

God's Envisioned Reality for Our Church
"Joy & Unity in Jesus to the Glory of God"

Our Church's Mission
"Followers of Jesus Sent into the World"

Church-Specific Mission Statement

Our Church's Current Reality

Our Church's Current Mission Focus

| consistencies | inconsistencies | consistencies | inconsistencies |

In order to move toward Jesus' envisioned reality for our church. . .
. . what must we maintain?   . . what must we crucify?   . . what must we create?

Goals relative to
Behaviors (how we act)

Goals relative to
Programs (what we do)

Strategies & Action Plans

Actions needed to **NURTURE** Jesus' Followers	Actions needed to **EQUIP** Jesus' Followers
Desired Outcomes	Desired Outcomes

Step 1: Align Your Church with Jesus' Vision

Step 2: Develop Mission Statement Specific to Your Church

Step 3: Assess Your Church's Current Reality & Current Mission Focus

Step 4: Identify Consistencies & Inconsistencies Between Envisioned & Current Realities

Step 5: Organize Your Church's Response

Suggested Communications

Possible Newsletter Article/Bulletin Inserts

Initial Communication

There is exciting news to share about our church! We are preparing to enter a process of spiritual engagement that will affect the future of our ministry and mission. Through a six-week Bible-study series entitled, *Does Your Church Have a Prayer? In Mission toward the Promised Land,* people in our congregation will gather in small Bible-study groups designed to allow their voices to be heard. A strategic-ministry planning task force has formed to help our church discern how we can live in the reality of Jesus' prayer for our church. Members of this task force are (insert names).

Based on the understanding that Jesus' prayer for his disciples in John 17 includes the people who are part of our fellowship, we will consider how we can live into the reality of Jesus' prayer for our church. You are invited to allow your voice to be heard as you travel this journey of faith with your church through prayer, participation in a small study group, worship, and other times of gathering. If you would like your voice to be heard, please respond to this invitation by calling the church office.

Small groups will be organized based on availability and preferred times. This letter includes a covenant card. As a symbol of your willingness to partic-ipate, we invite you to place your card on the altar at our service of consecration on _____. Will you join your friends in this time of personal renewal and congregational vision for our church?

Bible Study Invitation

Does Our Church Have a Prayer? six-week, church-wide, small-group Bible studies are being planned as we continue a process of spiritual engagement for our congregation. These Bible studies will help people in our church live in the vision of joy and unity in Jesus to the glory of God and in the mission of being followers of Jesus sent into the world. Through these studies, your voice will be heard as our church's strategic-ministry task force (Promised Land Task Force) prepares its report for our congregation. Current study groups are invited to engage in this Bible study. If you are not in a study group but would like to participate in this congregation-wide Bible study, contact (provide appropriate contact information for your church) by _____.

Invitation for Mission-Statement Team Presentation

Does Our Church Have a Prayer? This is the question that is being answered through a strategic-ministry planning process that is helping the voice of people throughout our church to be heard. On _____, potential mission statements for our church will be presented for congregational reflection and feedback. You are invited to attend this important meeting as your voice is heard in the formation of our church's strategic-ministry plan.

Invitation for Task-Force Presentation

Does Our Church Have a Prayer? The strategic-ministry plan task force will present a proposed strategic-ministry plan for our church on _____. You are invited to attend this presentation so that your voice may be heard.

"Helping Your Voice to Be Heard" Data Compilation

One of the responsibilities of the Data Coordinator is to compile small-group Bible-study responses from the sets of questions entitled "Helping Your Voice to Be Heard." The Bible study leaders will provide these data weekly as they collect responses from the participants in their Bible study groups. Each week, the Data Coordinator will combine all of the responses from the Bible study groups using the form provided here. When all responses are compiled, a team selected by the task force will have the responsibility for interpreting the current reality of your church based on these responses.

Bible Study One: Does Your Church Have a Prayer?

Number of Responses
1. Would you consider your church to be a praying church?
    a. _____Yes
    b. _____No

2. Is your church a joyful place?
    a. _____Yes
    b. _____No

3. Does a common vision that glorifies God unite your church?
    a. _____Yes
    b. _____No

4. Do people believe in Jesus because of your church?
    a. _____Yes
    b. _____No

5. Does your church make God's love known?
    a. _____Yes
    b. _____No

6. Does your church have a vision and/or mission statement?
    a. _____Yes
    b. _____No
    c. _____Don't know

7. If your church has a vision and/or mission statement, do you think it reflects the mission of Jesus' prayer for his disciples as noted in question three of "Questions for Scriptural Reflection?"
    a. _____Yes
    b. _____No

8. Which question would generate the most discussion at your church?
    a. _____Who has the keys to which doors at your church?
    b. _____How can we open the doors of our church to our community?

Bible Study Two: What Reality Do You Choose?

Number of Responses
1. I have observed murmuring in our church and have found it to be:
    a. _____Significantly detrimental.
    b. _____Somewhat detrimental.
    c. _____Minimally detrimental.
    d. _____Not at all detrimental.

2. Does your church have a history of honestly assessing its current reality?
    a. _____Yes
    b. _____No
    c. _____Don't know

3. Are issues at your church are decided through:
   a. _____Envisioned reality.
   b. _____Perceived reality.

4. Your church's past experience and history:
   a. _____Hold you back.
   b. _____Move you forward.

5. Today in our church:
   a. _____Most people choose to focus on the challenges that are facing our church as did the ten spies.
   b. _____Most people choose to focus on the promise of God's presence for our church as did Joshua and Caleb.

6. Does your church understand that it stands on the edge of God's Promised Land for Jesus' disciples?
   a. _____Yes
   b. _____No
   c. _____Don't know

Bible Study Three: Overcoming Giants

Number of Responses
1. Can your church name the giants that are preventing you from entering God's Promised Land of joy and unity?
   a. _____Yes
   b. _____No

2. Does your church focus more on the giants that are facing it than on God's vision for the future?
   a. _____Focus more on the giants
   b. _____Focus more on God's vision for the future

3. Has your church demonstrated the courage to make intentional choices that will empower it to overcome the giants that are facing it?
   a. _____Yes
   b. _____No

4. Would your community consider your church to be relevant to the present challenges of life?
   a. _____Yes
   b. _____No
   c. _____Don't know

5. What are the current giants that are facing your church?
   a. _____Lack of age diversity in the congregation
   b. _____A changing neighborhood
   c. _____Financial challenges
   d. _____Aging facility
   e. _____Changes in the number of church members
   f. _____Worship attendance
   g. _____History of conflict
   h. _____Other (List responses below)
   _____
   _____

6. What are strengths within your congregation that can help your church to overcome the giants it faces?
   a. _____Worship
   b. _____Location
   c. _____Spiritual formation opportunities
   d. _____Mission
   e. _____Church facility
   f. _____Financial strength
   g. _____Communication

Bible Study Four: Asking the Right Questions

Number of Responses
1. Would you say that "hallway conversations" at your church are usually meant to:
   a. _____Gain understanding?
   b. _____Complain?
   c. _____Resolve conflict?
   d. _____Accuse and blame?

2. Do questions in your church tend to:
    _____Build community.
    _____Destroy relationships.

3. Jesus asked his disciples, "What were you discussing on the way?" What does your church spend time discussing? (Pick four.)
    a. _____Present ministries
    b. _____The past
    c. _____Future ministries
    d. _____Who Jesus is
    e. _____Who's right or who's wrong
    f. _____Spreading the Good News
    g. _____What happened on Sunday
    h. _____Finances
    i. _____Lay leadership
    j. _____Staff leadership
    k. _____Concerns of your church
    l. _____Concerns of your community
    m. _____Defining your church's ministry
    n. _____Long-term survival
    o. _____Disappointing ministries
    p. _____Successful ministries
    q. _____How to get more people involved
    r. _____Worship attendance

4. What labels have you heard in your church? (Pick three.)
    a. _____Those new members
    b. _____Those old timers
    c. _____Us
    d. _____Them
    e. _____Involved
    f. _____Uninvolved
    g. _____Committed
    h. _____Non-committed

5. Does your congregation focuses on:
    a. _____Power struggles.
    b. _____Ministry.

6. Does your church have questions about its future?
   a. _____Yes
   b. _____No
   c. _____Don't know

7. Do questions in your church invite dialogue from diverse opinions?
   a. _____Yes
   b. _____No
   c. _____Don't know

8. Does the history of your church reflect power struggles that it continues to repeat?
   a. _____Yes
   b. _____No
   c. _____Don't know

9. Is there agreement or disagreement about what your congregation values most?
   a. _____Agreement
   b. _____Disagreement
   c. _____Don't know

Bible Study Five: Beyond and Within

Number of Responses
1. Your church's approach to ministry is focused on:
   a. _____Beyond.
   b. _____Within.

2. Do disagreements within your congregation tend to:
   a. _____Be resolved in ways that are effective
   b. _____Be resolved in ways that cause discord

3. Disagreements at our church are usually:
   a. _____Resolved quickly by consensus.
   b. _____Resolved quickly by one or two key leaders.
   c. _____Resolved quickly by the pastor or church staff.
   d. _____Avoided and unresolved.

4. Do you believe your church practices the pattern of conflict resolution that was practiced by the Jerusalem church?
   a. _____Yes
   b. _____No

5. Is your church united in its vision?
   a. _____Yes
   b. _____No

6. Does your congregation clearly understand its mission?
   a. _____Yes
   b. _____No

7. Disagreements in your church tend to:
   a. _____Linger.
   b. _____Be discussed openly.
   c. _____Cause hard feelings.
   d. _____Help your congregation to understand more clearly its mission.
   e. _____Polarize your congregation.
   f. _____Lead to new ways of thinking.
   g. _____Lead to new ministries.
   h. _____Result in blaming and frustration.
   i. _____Result in God's love being seen.

8. Do current ministries in your church invite people to see beyond self-focused concerns?
   a. _____Yes
   b. _____No
   c. _____Don't know

Bible Study Six: Entering God's Promised Land

Number of Responses
1. When our church has to make a choice, we:
   a. _____Are guided by a unified vision
   b. _____Get bogged down in details

2. Our church makes intentional choices about its ministries and mission:
   a. _____Yes
   b. _____No
   c. _____Don't know

3. Once the church makes a decision, the tendency in our church is for people to:
   a. _____Harbor hard feelings.
   b. _____Work behind the scenes creating discord.
   c. _____Support church decisions they may not personally agree with.
   d. _____Create faction of self-interest.
   e. _____Define decisions as winning or losing.

4. Are there new expressions of ministry in your church?
   a. _____Yes
   b. _____No
   c. _____Don't know

5. Most of our church programs focus on:
   a. _____The needs of our members.
   b. _____The needs of our surrounding community.

6. I believe that because Jesus prayed for our church, our church has a prayer and can enter God's Promised Land for Jesus' disciples:
   a. _____Yes
   b. _____No

FaithFull Journey, LLC.*
Current Reality Profile^{SM}

Through the Bible-study series and church/community demographic data analysis, FaithFull Journey, LLC offers churches the opportunity to hear and understand their current reality. Congregational members engage in the education and discussion of the scriptural foundations of strategic-ministry planning. In the context of those scriptural foundations, they answer questions relative to current church reality. The data are compiled, analyzed, and presented in a graphical, ready-to-use PowerPoint presentation. The package presents a clear picture of your surrounding community and the broad-based opinions of your congregation detailing the alignment of your church to the vision and mission of Jesus' prayer for his disciples. Areas that will be addressed include:

- Do we have a mission?
- Is our mission clear?
- Where do we currently focus our efforts?
- What has our history been?
- How do we behave toward each other?
- How do we make decisions?

- What are our major strengths?
- What impact are we having?
- What are the giants that face our church (our biggest obstacles)?

For further information, contact www.FaithfullJourney.org or write to:

FaithFull Journey, LLC
P.O. Box 1473
Midlothian, VA 23113

About the Authors

Marc Brown is the Director of Connectional Ministries for the Virginia Conference of the United Methodist Church. Ordained in 1977, Marc has served as the pastor of a variety of churches and as a district superintendent. Marc's ministry focuses on missional church revitalization.

Kathy Ashby Merry pursued her calling to the world of church work after retiring, at age forty-two, from a whirlwind business career. As a senior operations executive for a large health insurance company, she was devoted to transforming business processes for the benefit of the company, its employees, and customers. Kathy now applies her organizational development skills for the advancement of God's work.

John Briggs, a retired business executive, entered the ministry at age forty-nine. His interest and experience in company "turn-arounds" and expansion provide a unique foundation for church renewal and growth. John presently serves a pastoral appointment in the Virginia Conference.